C000182710

The History of My Going for Refuge

Reflections on the Occasion of the Twentieth Anniversary of the Western Buddhist Order (Triratna Buddhist Order)

Sangharakshita

Windhorse Publications

Published by
Windhorse Publications Ltd.
169 Mill Road
Cambridge
CB1 3AN, UK
info@windhorsepublications.com
www.windhorsepublications.com

© Sangharakshita 1988

First published 1988
Second edition 2010

Cover design by Stefanie Ine Grewe. Initial concept by
Peter Wenman
Author photograph by Alokavira/Timm Sonnenschein,
www.timmsonnenschein.com
Printed by Bell & Bain Ltd., Glasgow

British Library Cataloguing in Publication Data:
A catalogue record for this book is available from the
British Library

ISBN: 9781 907314 00 1
ISSN: 2042-0560

Mixed Sources
Product group from well-managed
forests and other controlled sources
www.fsc.org Cert no. TT-COC-002769
© 1996 Forest Stewardship Council

FSC

Contents

Preface to the Second Edition

This slender volume, with its unassuming title, holds a wealth of spiritual insight and teaching. In it, Sangharakshita traces his growing understanding of the essential nature of what it is to live and practise a Buddhist life. Being essential, it is also universal and applies throughout time, culture and individual lifestyle: it is the act of Going for Refuge to the Buddha, Dharma and Sangha.

But what is Going for Refuge? It is fundamentally a *movement*: a movement towards what has value and away from what restricts us; a movement which mirrors the even more basic process of life and growth. Plants and trees growing towards the light and the sun; one life form evolving into another; the sometimes inchoate intimations and stirrings in ourselves towards what we sense to be more meaningful and significant. Sangharakshita has described elsewhere the principle of Going for Refuge as 'to allow oneself to be attracted towards the best and the highest with which one is in personal contact.'

At the time that Sangharakshita ordained the first twelve men and women into the Western Buddhist Order (now the Triratna Buddhist Order) and by doing so founded a new Buddhist Order, I was a young student at a northern university studying for a degree in philosophy. Questions about the meaning of life had arisen early for me. My upbringing was atheist, so God and conventional religion held no truth for me. My parents divorced while I was still a child, so marriage and family were not likely to be the answer. Socialism seemed to offer some solution, but the Cuba crisis in my teenage years and the very real threat of nuclear annihilation brought even that strongly into question. Philosophy at least addressed the questions of meaning and truth head-on, and I thought that here at least I would be able to find the basis for a true direction in life. I got into my studies with the natural enthusiasm of a young woman in the Britain of the late sixties for whom the world was opening up, and with confidence that I could find the pearl in the oyster.

I can remember the moment of disenchantment when the 'consolations of philosophy' proved insufficient; can remember even my position in the seminar group, the angle of my chair. It was a seminar on Wittgenstein and I was feeling the excitement, pleasure and – it must be said – pride of following the philosophical propositions of an extraordinarily acute mind when I caught sight, through the glass partition, of one of the cleaning staff walking down the corridor with a broom. In that moment far more than a glass partition separated our two worlds. I felt the acute lack of being able to translate these philosophical truths into any form that would have relevance to her life or to the lives of millions of others, so that the heightened sense of their significance collapsed along with my excitement and pride.

Within a week of finishing my degree I sold almost all my course books and most of my possessions and went to live with friends in the west of Ireland, in a commune dedicated to going 'back to the land'. With the breakdown of the commune a couple of years later, I travelled overland to India – like many of my generation, seeking truth in a more overtly spiritual culture. I returned, a year older and two stones lighter, to the unexpected shock of arriving back in the West and feeling a sense of alienation from my own culture. The stimulus of the emerging feminist movement, a consciousness-raising group, and working with disadvantaged children saved me from depression.

I can't say that I was attracted towards the 'best and highest' in my experience during those years, but I was certainly in search of meaning, blessed with a certain determination and in need of refuge. It would be another five years before I met the Dharma and the Sangha Jewels, and a further nine years before my own Going for Refuge to the Three Jewels was witnessed at the time of my ordination ceremony.

The need for refuge arises out of our existential situation, our humanity. Experiences in life are a mixture of pain and pleasure, sometimes a bewildering mixture: of suffering and loss, love and beauty. Within this maelstrom is the deep desire, more or less conscious, for security of some kind; for meaning, truth, guidance; something by which we can steer a course through the vicissitudes of life.

One of the earliest Buddhist texts, the *Dhammapada*, states this dilemma:

> Many people, out of fear, flee for refuge to sacred hills, woods, groves, trees and shrines. In reality this is not a safe refuge. In reality this is not the best refuge. Fleeing to such a refuge one is not released from all suffering.

The 'sacred groves' of the present age take a different form. Celebrity culture comes to mind, defying the ageing process, conspicuous wealth, the perfect relationship, peak experiences – these are all 'false refuges' because they do not address the underlying anxiety of human life.

> One who goes for refuge to the Enlightened One, to the Truth and to the Spiritual Community ... this is a safe refuge, this is the best refuge. Having gone to such a refuge one is released from all suffering.

The Buddha, Dharma and Sangha offer a true refuge because they are both one with Reality and with what we can become: the ever-present potential for growth, the truth about existence, and the depth of human and spiritual connection with others. There is also that resonance of something deeply intuited but not consciously known which is often described as a 'coming home'. It can be the sense of compassion evoked by an image of the Buddha, hearing a teaching of the Dharma that seems incontrovertible, or simply contact with the Sangha, a living community. It is the intuitive sense of wanting to be in relationship with something that goes beyond one's own limitations and yet is somehow in accord with one's deepest nature. Traditionally the three Refuges are chanted before any session of spiritual practice:

Buddham saranam gacchami
Dhammam saranam gacchami
Sangham saranam gacchami

To the Buddha for Refuge I go
To the Dhamma for Refuge I go
To the Sangha for Refuge I go

We do not go for Refuge once, or only on ceremonial occasions, but over and over again. It becomes a way of life: we become 'Going for Refuge beings', revealing the creative and radical nature of this activity.

In the creative process something is brought into being, given form, clarified by being acted upon.

Our understanding and feeling for the three Refuges develops through the 'going', the movement towards them. Simultaneously, that action has an effect on our being: we become, momentarily at least, less ego-centred, and in turn our motivation is purified. To paraphrase Jung: it is not Shakespeare who creates Lear, but Lear who creates Shakespeare. What may have begun as a desire to 'be happy' becomes a wish to identify more deeply both with the joys and with the sorrows of others. What begins as a wish for superficial 'equanimity', a sort of invulnerability, becomes an appreciation of experiencing everything more fully. The aspiration to 'help others' becomes a recognition of the need to change oneself. The desire for perfection becomes an acknowledgement of our humanness, and thereby a greater sense of empathy with others. The momentum to move towards the Three Jewels of Refuge continues, but the change that needs to happen in that movement clarifies and becomes more authentic.

Going for Refuge is radical because it places no limitations on how far we can take our practice; even the level of 'absolute' Going for Refuge, or Enlightenment itself, is not an end but an ongoing flowering of the creative mind. It is radical also because it cuts through any cultural accretions which the Buddhist tradition may have acquired and which can stultify genuine spiritual practice, revealing in its apparent simplicity both beauty and depth. Only I can go for Refuge; no one can act as intermediary or on my behalf. It is a conscious volition involving action and change. One can't 'take' Refuge, despite the action sometimes being described in this way. The verb is 'gacchami': 'I go'. It is an active process, not something one can appropriate. At the same time it provides a constant source of guidance: in each moment there is the Buddha Jewel (our aspiration to grow), the Dharma Jewel (the next step), and the Sangha Jewel (the opportunity for communication and connection).

In this 'History' Sangharakshita has given us the remarkable gift of a coherent perspective on the whole Buddhist tradition. He has made it clear that 'there are no higher teachings, only deeper understandings.' Going for Refuge is not simply a preliminary practice which is superseded by more 'advanced' practices; one continues to go for Refuge at deeper and deeper levels of understanding and experience, or equally it could be said, with greater and greater commitment and devotion to the Three Jewels of Refuge. From his emphasis on its centrality emerges his unique exposition of the levels of Going for Refuge, providing a coherent map of the spiritual journey: a journey that begins simply with the initial response of being drawn to the values of the Buddha, his teachings and the community of practitioners. The ongoing commitment to, and living out of, those values can be transformative, giving rise to Insight into the nature of existence and culminating in the active compassion and wisdom of Enlightenment. At this point one has become those Refuges. The act of Going for Refuge has become a non-egoic stream of spiritual energy directed for the benefit of all beings.

Sangharakshita's clarification of Going for Refuge as 'the central and definitive act of a Buddhist life' and 'what makes a Buddhist a Buddhist' has that simplicity and elegance of truth, of getting to the heart of the matter, which is the characteristic of an unusually creative and singular mind. And it is fascinating to see that understanding unfold through the particularities of his own spiritual journey: the initial Insight on reading the *Diamond Sutra* that he was a Buddhist and always had been one; the longing and determination to commit himself to a full Buddhist life through ordination as a monk; the 'surrender' to his teacher to stay in Kalimpong 'for the good of Buddhism', continuing to practice independently through periods of disappointment and struggle. And there's the synchronicity of that time in meeting with his Tibetan Mahayana and Vajrayana teachers together with the encounter with the great Dr Ambedkar, who initially made the remarkable request of this young English monk to lead the ceremony of conversion to Buddhism for hundreds of thousands of Indian Dalits inhumanly oppressed by the caste system.

Throughout all those years Sangharakshita has needed to ask himself searching questions: What does it mean to be a Buddhist and live a Buddhist life? What does it mean to practice the Dharma? What is the meaning of 'conversion' to Buddhism? It is out of deep reflection, together with those meetings with different Buddhist traditions and remarkable individuals, that this apparently simple yet all-embracing teaching of the centrality of Going for Refuge emerges.

And one last word from Sangharakshita on the subject can only increase our fascination with this profound but immediate act: that Going for Refuge is no less than 'the key to the mystery of existence'.

Maitreyi
Tiratanaloka, April 2010

To discover that within myself which I must obey, to gain some awareness of the law which operates in the organic whole of the internal world, to feel this internal world as an organic whole working out its whole destiny according to some secret vital principle, to know which acts and utterances are a liberation from obstacles and an accession of strength, to acknowledge secret loyalties which one cannot deny without impoverishment and starvation – this is to possess one's soul indeed, and it is not easy either to do or to explain.

John Middleton Murry (1889–1957)

1
Introduction

Today marks the twentieth anniversary of the Western Buddhist Order [renamed the Triratna Buddhist Order in 2010], which came into existence on Sunday, 7 April 1968, when, in the course of a ceremony held at Centre House, London, nine men and three women committed themselves to the Path of the Buddha by publicly 'taking' the Three Refuges and Ten Precepts from me in the traditional manner. In the terse phrases of the diary that I kept for the first three and a half months of that year, and which has only recently come to light:

> Arrived at Centre House at 10.15. Found nothing ready. Cleared and arranged room, set up shrine etc. People started coming, including bhikkhus. Started at 11.15. Welcome by Jack [Austin]. Had lunch with bhikkhus and Jack while Mike Rogers conducted first meditation. Emile [Boin] very worried, as Indians who had undertaken to provide lunch did not turn up until very late. At 12 o'clock spoke on 'The Idea of the Western Buddhist Order and

the Upasaka Ordination'. Then, while others were having lunch, spoke to the press. Many photographs taken. Guided group discussion. Meditation. Tea. More press people and more photographs. At 5.30 spoke on 'The Bodhisattva Vow'. At 7 o'clock conducted ordination ceremony, which lasted till 8.15. Mike Ricketts, Mike Rogers, Sara [Boin], Emile [Boin], Terry O'Regan, Stephen [Parr], Marghareta [Kahn], Geoffrey [Webster], John Hipkin, Roy Brewer, Penny [Neild-Smith], and David Waddell received their [public] ordinations. Everything went off very smoothly and successfully. All most pleased.

A further (visual) record of the occasion is provided by four colour slides taken by my friend Terry Delamare. The first slide is a close up of the shrine, the centre of which is occupied by a sedent bronze image of Amitayus, the Buddha of Infinite Life, flanked by slightly smaller images of Avalokitesvara, the Bodhisattva of Compassion, and Manjugosha, the Bodhisattva of Wisdom. Behind the images is a miniature Japanese screen of white silk brocade; in front, an arrangement of white carnations, irises, lilies, and narcissi. The second and third slides show me giving one or other of my lectures, while in the fourth and last I am about to place the white kesa of the Order round the neck of Sara Boin (Sujata), who kneels on a cushion before me with joined hands. Since the seven other members of the Order who appear in the slide are not wearing kesas, Sara may well have been the first person to be ordained.

Immediately after the ceremony I hurriedly dismantled the shrine and with Stephen (Ananda) caught the 9.50 train to Haslemere, where we spent four tranquil days at a semi-derelict cottage in the extensive grounds of Quartermaine, and where I worked on my memoirs and wrote a few 'Chinese' poems. One of these poems read:

Beyond the deserted paddock, a dark wood;
Before our secluded cottage, wet strips of green
*   and brown.*
Watching the incense burn in this quiet room
We have forgotten the passing of days and hours.

We were not allowed to forget them for long, however. On the afternoon of the fourth day Ananda had to return to London and to his work as a recording engineer at Bush House, while I had to go over to Keffolds – the Ockenden Venture's other property in Haslemere – and lead the FWBO Easter retreat. This retreat was attended by several of the new Order members, some of whom indeed made themselves useful in various ways. The Western Buddhist Order had not only come into existence but had started functioning.

But what was this Western Buddhist Order – or Trailokya Bauddha Mahasangha, as it was subsequently known in India – that after a year or more of preliminary work had suddenly blossomed lotus-like from the mud of the metropolis? Essentially it was a body of people who had gone for Refuge to the Buddha, the Dharma, and the Sangha and who, by virtue of that common spiritual commitment, now constituted a spiritual community – a spiritual community that symbolized, on the mundane level, the same transcendental Spiritual Community or Sangha which was the third of those same Three Jewels to which they had gone for Refuge. Moreover, the twelve people who made up the Western Buddhist Order had not only gone for Refuge to the Three Jewels: they had 'taken' the Refuges and Precepts from me or had, in other words, been ordained by me. Their understanding of what was meant by Going for Refuge must therefore have coincided with mine, at least to some extent. In what sense, then, did I myself Go for Refuge? How did I understand that central and definitive act of the Buddhist life, and how had I arrived at that understanding? On an occasion like this, when we have assembled in (relatively) large numbers to celebrate the twentieth anniversary of the spiritual community that forms the heart of the new Buddhist movement we have inaugurated, it is no doubt appropriate that I should cast a backward glance over the various stages by which the meaning, the significance, and the

4

importance of Going for Refuge became clear to me. It is no doubt appropriate that I should endeavour to trace the history of my Going for Refuge, and that, having done this, I should share with you some of my current thinking as regards my own relation to the Order and the relation of the Order itself to the rest of the Buddhist world.

In tracing the history of my Going for Refuge I shall not simply be tracing a series of logical deductions from – or even of more and more extensive practical applications of – a concept or principle comprehended in its fullness, and in all its bearings, from the very beginning. My progression here has resembled that of Yeats' butterfly rather than that of his gloomy bird of prey. Indeed, in order to make clear what follows, or at least avoid misunderstandings, at this point it becomes necessary for me to say a few words about my personal psychology. Some years ago an astrologer friend drew my birth chart, and according to this chart I had most of my planets below the horizon, which apparently meant that the influences which these planets represented were operating not in the field of consciousness but below it.[1] Though I have never taken astrology very seriously, or indeed had any real interest in the subject, reflecting on this fact I nonetheless came to the conclusion that the course of my life had been determined by impulse and intuition rather than by reason and logic and that, for me, there could be no question of first clarifying an idea or concept and then acting upon it, i.e. acting upon it in its clarified form. An idea or concept was clarified in the process of its being acted upon. This was certainly what happened in the case of my Going for Refuge. The full significance of that supremely important act became apparent to me only gradually as, over the years, I acted upon the imperfect idea of Going for Refuge which I already had, and as, my idea of it being clarified to some extent, I again acted upon it and it was again clarified – the act becoming more adequate to the idea as the idea itself became clearer, and the idea becoming clearer as the act became more adequate. In tracing the history of my Going for Refuge, therefore, I shall be tracing the history of a process of discovery which follows a rather erratic course and which consists, besides, of a series of slow, sometimes virtually imperceptible developments wherein are no dramatic breakthroughs except, perhaps, at the very beginning. So slow and so little perceptible, indeed, were some of those developments, that they can be discerned only with difficulty, so that it is fortunate that some of them found expression – either at the time or shortly afterwards – in certain of my writings, lectures, and seminars. In the case of the first of the various stages by which the meaning, the significance, and the importance of Going for Refuge became clear to me, no such *aide-mémoires* are necessary. After more than forty-five years the experience retains its original freshness for me, at least when I call it to mind and dwell upon it.

2

The *Diamond Sutra* and the *Sutra of Wei Lang*

The experience with which the history of my Going for Refuge begins took place in the late summer or early autumn of 1942, when I was sixteen or seventeen, and it took place as a result of my reading the *Diamond Sutra* and the *Sutra of Wei Lang (Hui Neng)*, especially the former. I have described this crucial experience in my memoirs of the period, written in the late fifties, and since I am unable to improve upon the account I then gave I shall simply quote from the first part of it.[2] Speaking of my initial response to the *Diamond Sutra*, I wrote: 'Though this book epitomizes a teaching of such rarefied sublimity that even Arhats, saints who have attained individual nirvana, are said to become confused and afraid when they hear of it for the first time, I at once joyfully embraced it with an unqualified acceptance and assent. To me the truth taught by the Buddha in the *Diamond Sutra* was not new. I had known and believed and realized it ages before, and the reading of the sutra as it were awoke me to the existence of something I had

7

forgotten. Once I realized that I was a Buddhist it seemed that I had always been one, that it was the most natural thing in the world to be one, and that I had never been anything else.' After offering two possible explanations for my feeling that I had always been a Buddhist I went on to describe my experience of the *Sutra of Wei Lang* which, I wrote, threw me into 'a kind of ecstasy' whenever I read it. The truth taught by the Buddha in the *Diamond Sutra* and to a more limited extent by the Sixth Patriarch in the *Sutra of Wei Lang* was, of course, the highest truth of Buddhism (so far as that truth can be expressed in words), the truth of Shunyata or 'Voidness' – the truth, that is to say, that the phenomena of existence are ultimately non-different from Absolute Reality, and Absolute Reality ultimately non-different from the phenomena of existence. Such being the case, the fact that I had responded so positively and unreservedly to this teaching meant that my Dharma-eye had been opened, at least to some extent, and that as a result of my reading of the *Diamond Sutra* and the *Sutra of Wei Lang* I had in fact gone for Refuge to the Dharma, the second of the Three Jewels.

Whether I also went for Refuge to the first and third of the Three Jewels as a result of my reading the two sutras, and, if so, whether I went for Refuge to them in the same way that I did to the second, is another question. I was certainly aware that the truth taught in the *Diamond Sutra* had been taught by the

8

Buddha and that, although its immediate recipient was the Arhant Subhuti, it had in fact been addressed to an assembly of monks and Bodhisattvas representing the Spiritual Community or Sangha. I was even aware that in the *Sutra of Wei Lang* the sixth Patriarch had exhorted his listeners to take refuge in the Three Jewels of their 'essence of mind' (as Wong Mow Lam translated the expression). Nevertheless, so overwhelmed was I by what the *Diamond Sutra* itself calls 'the impact of the Dharma' that for the time being I was virtually oblivious to the existence of the Buddha and the Sangha. Indeed, were it not for the fact that both the Buddha and the Sangha are ultimately non-different from Shunyata it might be said that, so far as I was concerned, the first and third of the Three Jewels had both been swallowed up by the Void!

But though for the time being I was oblivious to the existence of the first and third Jewels, I had long been fascinated by the life and personality of the Buddha. Three or four years before my encounter with the *Diamond Sutra* and the *Sutra of Wei Lang* I had, in fact, written a 'Life of Siddhartha Gautama the Buddha', as I called it. This little work I compiled mainly from the *Children's Encyclopaedia* and H. G. Wells' *A Short History of the World*, and it is perhaps significant that, apart from school essays, it was my first completed piece of writing. At about the same time I bought, at a curio shop in Brighton, a small brass Kamakura Buddha in which – the top of its head being perforated for the purpose – I regularly burned joss sticks. This act of devotion did not in itself amount to Going for Refuge, of course, any more than did the writing of my 'Life of Siddhartha Gautama the Buddha', but at least it showed that I had a feeling for the Buddha that I certainly did not have for the Sangha or Spiritual Community. After my realization that I was a Buddhist nearly two years, in fact, were to pass before I made personal contact with other Buddhists, and two years and a few months before I formally went for Refuge to all Three Jewels.

3
U Thittila and Pansil

These other Buddhists with whom I made personal contact, in the winter of 1943-44, were the members of the Buddhist Society, founded in London in 1924 by Christmas Humphreys as the Buddhist Lodge of the Theosophical Society. By the time I made contact with them I had been conscripted into the army, but I attended meetings whenever I could and struck up acquaintance with a few people. At one of these meetings (it may have been a Wesak meeting, but I cannot be sure) I found myself 'taking Pansil', as it was called, from an orange-robed figure seated behind a table at the far end of the room. 'Pansil' was the Sinhalese corruption of the Pali 'Pancha Sila' or 'Five Precepts', and one 'took Pansil' by repeating the Five Precepts, preceded by the Three Refuges, after whoever happened to be conducting the ceremony. Though many of the circumstances of that meeting have long faded from my mind, I have vivid recollections of myself and some fifteen or twenty other people standing in our places with our Pansil cards in our hands as, with varying degrees of uncertainty with regard to the pronunciation of the unfamiliar

Pali words, we followed a clear-voiced and confident Christmas Humphreys as he led us in the chanting of the responses. Most vivid of all is the recollection of looking down at the Pansil card I held in my own two hands. Even now I can see the oblong of shining white card on which the Refuges and Precepts were printed in both Pali and English. Even now I can hear the voice of Christmas Humphreys pronouncing the 'dutiyampis' and 'tatiyampis' of the Refuge-going formula in a way that, to my unaccustomed ear, seemed to bear little relation to the words as printed.

The orange-robed figure from whom I had 'taken Pansil', and whose guttural tones had been too low for me to catch, was the Burmese monk U Thittila. He was the first Buddhist monk I had seen and, in view of some of the developments which, many years later, took place in my own life and thought as a Buddhist, it was significant that it was he, rather than a more 'orthodox' representative of Eastern Buddhism, who conducted the ceremony whereat I recited for the first time the formula which, publicly repeated after a leading Buddhist, constitutes 'conversion' to Buddhism and formal acceptance into the Buddhist community. It was significant that it was U Thittila who conducted the ceremony because, though on this occasion he wore the robes of the branch of the Theravada Monastic Order to which he belonged, he did not always wear them. On less formal occasions, as when he was out with the ARP, he wore whatever form of Western dress was appropriate. Years later, when I was myself 'in the robes', I learned that this 'unorthodox' behaviour had not met with universal approval. As I wrote in my unpublished memoirs, 'Narrowly formalistic Burmese Buddhists had severely criticized him for his supposed misconduct in wearing ordinary European clothes when not actually performing his religious duties. English Buddhists saw the matter in quite a different light. Throughout the Blitz U Thittila had worked as a stretcher-bearer, on several occasions risking his life to rescue people trapped under fallen masonry. Finding that the voluminous drapery of his robes hampered his movements he sensibly exchanged them for more practical garments. People who knew him said he practised what he preached.' For my own part, I have always been glad that I first took the Refuges and Precepts from this quiet and unassuming man for whom, as we now say, commitment was primary and lifestyle secondary – a man who, whether wearing orange robes or a blue boiler-suit, was at heart neither monk nor layman, but simply a Buddhist.

4
Going Forth

Between my 'taking Pansil' from U Thittila and my 'Going Forth' there was an interval of more than three years. During that period the Signals Unit to which I belonged had been ordered overseas, I had been stationed in Delhi, Colombo, Calcutta, and Singapore, had made contact with Chinese and Sinhalese Buddhists, had returned to India (for good, as I then thought), had been associated with various religious organizations and groups, both Buddhist and Hindu, and had taken up the regular practice of meditation. Now I was ready to enter upon the next of the various stages by which the meaning, the significance, and the importance of Going for Refuge became clear to me, and accordingly, on 18 August 1947 (three days after the Union Jack ceased to flutter over the Indian subcontinent and eight days before my twenty-second birthday), in Kasauli in East Punjab, I renounced the household life and went forth into the life of homelessness. The immediate cause of my taking this drastic step was disillusionment with worldly life, especially with worldly life as represented by organized religion. Together

with the Bengali friend with whom, on my return
to India, I had joined forces, I had worked for the
Ramakrishna Mission Institute of Culture and for
the Maha Bodhi Society. More recently I had been
involved in a project for the revival of the Dharma
Vijaya Vahini, an organization for the propagation of
Buddhism in India that had been started, many years
earlier, by an old scholar whom I happened to meet
at an interreligious gathering in Ahmedabad. With all
these organizations, as well as with the group that had
formed round a well-known female ascetic, I had been
deeply disappointed, as had my friend. Working with
such bodies was, it seemed, a hindrance rather than
a help to spiritual development. They had a natural
tendency to degenerate, and the only course open to
us was to sever our connection not just with them
but also with the world. As related in that portion
of my memoirs which was published in 1976 as *The
Thousand-Petalled Lotus*, we therefore dyed our clothes
the traditional ochre, disposed of our worldly possessions, said goodbye to our friends, and the following
morning – the morning of the 18th – set out on foot
down the road that led from Kasauli to the plains.

In 'Going Forth' in this way we were, of course,
following an ancient Indian tradition – a tradition
that the Buddha himself had followed some twenty-
five centuries earlier. Indeed, both before and after
my companion and I took our plunge into the ocean
of the spiritual life instead of sitting hesitating on the

15

shore (to vary the metaphor), I was very conscious that in exchanging the household life for the life of homelessness we were following the personal example of the Buddha, as well as that of many of his closest followers, and the consciousness that we were so doing inspired and uplifted me. The Buddha's own 'Going Forth' had terminated at the foot of the Bodhi Tree, when he attained the Supreme Enlightenment that, for the last six years, had been the object of his 'noble quest'. So far as his followers were concerned (i.e. those of them who had 'Gone Forth' either before meeting him or after Going for Refuge to the Three Jewels as a result of hearing his teaching), some attained Enlightenment while others did not, depending on how faithfully they had followed the Path he had shown. As time went on, and especially after the Buddha's *parinirvana* or 'Great Decease', Going for Refuge, 'Going Forth', and even 'becoming a monk' in the later narrow, more formalistic sense, came to be more and more closely identified (just as the Sangha or Spiritual Community and the Monastic Order came to be more and more closely identified). The story of how this happened is a long one, and I have no time to tell it now. I mention the matter at all only because I want to make the point that at this stage in the history of my Going for Refuge I had not sorted these things out. Despite having taken Pansil from U Thittila I had not realized that Going for Refuge was the central and decisive, indeed the definitive, act of the Buddhist life (one did not Go for Refuge because one was a Buddhist but was a Buddhist because one went for Refuge), and that 'Going Forth' and 'becoming a monk' were spiritually of significance and value only to the extent that they were expressions of one's Going for Refuge. I had not realized that 'Going Forth', far from being simply a matter of renouncing the household life, in fact consisted in the emergence of the individual – in the sense of the self-aware, emotionally positive, and responsible human being (to name only a few of his or her characteristic qualities) – from the matrix of group or merely-collective existence.

Because I did not realize this latter point, for me, as for many Eastern Buddhists, the next step after 'Going Forth' (which in any case had been formalized as sramanera or 'novice' ordination) consisted not, as it should really have done, in finding and being accepted into a (spiritual) community of those who had both gone for Refuge and 'Gone Forth', so much as in taking bhikshu ordination and in this way entering into full membership of the Monastic Order. Thus it was not surprising that my companion and I, having 'Gone Forth', should not only want to study Buddhism but should also want to take ordination as bhikshus. Our original plan had been to study and, if possible, to take ordination, in Ceylon, and on reaching Delhi we had accordingly lost no time in heading south. On our arrival in Colombo, however, we were refused entry into Ceylon and were forced to return to South India where, after some interesting adventures, we eventually settled in a deserted ashram on the outskirts of the town of Muvattupuzha, in the State of Travancore, where we stayed for fifteen months.

Looking back over the years it is difficult not to feel that the failure of our original plan was in fact an instance of the proverbial blessing in disguise, since it is extremely unlikely that we should have found in Ceylon the right conditions for our spiritual development. During the period of our stay in Muvattupuzha the greater part of my time was spent in study, meditation, and reflection, and in this way I came to have a clearer understanding of the Dharma, especially of the Dharma as represented by the teachings of Dependent Origination (Conditioned Co-production), the Four Noble Truths, and the Three Characteristics of Conditioned Existence, as well as a keener awareness of the fact that I was a Buddhist. This keener awareness of my spiritual identity, as it may be termed, was due in part at least to the fact that throughout our stay in South India I was surrounded by Hindus of various castes and sects (the few Indian Christians did not really count) and had no contact with Buddhists whatever – for my companion, though in some respects appreciative of Buddhism, was by birth a Brahmin and had not yet completely freed himself from his Hindu conditioning. Indeed,

I had had no contact with Buddhists of any kind since my departure from the Maha Bodhi Society nearly two years earlier. Despite this prolonged spiritual isolation, however, my allegiance to Buddhism remained unshaken. If anything it was more firmly and deeply rooted than ever, so that by the time our stay in Muvattupuzha came to an end I was again thinking of ordination and thinking of it more seriously than ever, as indeed was my companion. Nevertheless, though I was again thinking of ordination, I still thought of it not in terms of finding and being accepted into a spiritual community but in terms of taking bhikshu ordination and joining the Monastic Order. In other words, I had not understood that for the Buddhist, at least, the act of 'Going Forth' was a transition from group or merely-collective existence as represented by the household life to supra-collective but associated existence as represented by the spiritual community. I had not understood this because I did not, at this stage, have a clear understanding of the difference between the group, consisting of those who are merely group members, and the spiritual community, consisting of those who are individuals in the sense I have indicated. Because I did not have a clear understanding of this vitally important difference, I was unable to envisage the possibility that in becoming a monk and joining the Monastic Order I might become, not a 'member' of a spiritual community, but only a member of *another*

19

kind of group – not a secular group but a religious or even an ecclesiastical group.

For my failure to understand the difference between the group and the spiritual community, the group member and the individual, I was not altogether to blame, for, as I came to appreciate only years later, it was a failure common to virtually the whole Buddhist world, many parts of which were sunk in monastic or pseudo-monastic formalism of an extreme kind. As I trace the early stages of this history of my Going for Refuge, therefore, I must be careful not to be too hard on my younger and less experienced self and careful not to expect too much of him. More important still, I must be careful lest I forget, or lose touch with, or even start underestimating, the mood of spiritual exaltation with which I renounced the household life and went forth into the homeless life. Our past selves underlie our present self, even as the Catacombs underlie modern Rome – or rather, they live on in our present self and in a sense actually form part of it. This is certainly the case with my 'Going Forth' in Kasauli and the period of seclusion at Muvattupuzha that followed. Indeed, despite the fact that I did not, at the time, understand the full significance of the step I was taking, I regard my 'Going Forth' as being not only one of the most important stages in the history of my Going for Refuge but one of the principal turning points in my life. For this reason, when I realized last year that the fortieth anniversary of my 'Going Forth' was approaching, I could not help feeling that I would like to commemorate the occasion in some way, if only by preparing a paper in which I would recall my 'Going Forth' and reflect on its significance. This did not prove practicable. I was still recovering from the effects of the operations I had undergone earlier in the year, besides being busy with the women's Ordination Retreat and the various Order Conventions. When 18 August came I found myself – most appropriately – at 'Guhyaloka', where I quietly celebrated the day on my own account. As I sat on the veranda of my bungalow, looking out over the bright green pine trees of our magical valley at the wall of grey rock immediately opposite, there flashed on my 'inward eye' the small hill station in distant India and my saffron-clad, 22-year-old self 'Going Forth' on that fateful morning all those years ago, and I mused on the step I had taken and on the consequences it had had for myself and others.

One of the thoughts that occurred to me, as I sat there in the sunshine, was that experiences like taking Pansil and 'Going Forth' were more than just stages in the long process of discovery whereby the meaning and significance of Going for Refuge had gradually become clear to me; each stage also possessed, quite apart from that process, an independent value and significance that ought to be appreciated for its own sake. But I have no time to pursue the implications

21

of this idea, or to consider its bearing on the actual discovery process, to the next stage of which I must now turn.

5
Sramanera Ordination

The scene of this next stage was Kusinara, the site of the Buddha's *parinirvana* or Great Decease, where my companion and I arrived a few days before Wesak, having walked all the way from Benares at the hottest time of year. As related at length in *The Thousand-Petalled Lotus*, we had left Muvattupuzha four or five months earlier and had gradually made our way north with the intention of visiting the Buddhist sacred places and, if possible, taking formal ordination as Buddhist monks. During this period my desire for contact with other Buddhists, already quite strong by the time of our departure from Muvattupuzha, had become unbearably intense. It had also become centred on Sarnath, where the Buddha had delivered his First Discourse and where, as I knew, there was a centre of the Maha Bodhi Society and a small monastic community. Here, then, we had presented ourselves – and here, to our bitter disappointment, we had been received with hostility and suspicion and had had our request for ordination turned down with flimsy excuses which were, we later discovered, little better than lies. On the advice of a scholar-monk in Benares whose disciple I subsequently became, we had therefore decided to seek ordination in Kusinara and, being entirely without money, had proceeded to make the hundred-mile journey on foot – an arduous and at that time of year a positively dangerous undertaking.

In Kusinara we fared better than we had done at Sarnath (we could hardly have fared worse). U Chandramani Maha Thera, the 72-year-old Burmese monk who had devoted his life to the restoration of the place, listened to our request for ordination sympathetically, asked a number of questions, promised to consider our request, and a few days later informed us that provided it was clearly understood that he could accept no responsibility for our future training, and that it would not be possible for us to stay with him at Kusinara, he was ready to ordain us. On Wesak morning, 12 May 1949, my companion and I therefore took ordination as sramaneras or novice monks by repeating after U Chandramani the Three Refuges and Ten Sramanera Precepts. For me the principal significance of the occasion was to be found in the re-establishment of my contact with other Buddhists (it had hardly been re-established at Sarnath), as well as in the formalization of my 'freelance' Going Forth of nearly two years ago and the consequent regularization of my hitherto ambiguous position within the (monastic) community – a regularization that would, I hoped, pave the way to my becoming a bhikshu. Thus although my desire for contact with other Buddhists was intense it lacked clarity, being in effect a desire not so much to find and be accepted into the spiritual community as to join the Monastic Order as such. The reason for this was that I was thinking, basically, in terms of 'becoming a monk' rather than in terms of Going for Refuge, having not yet realized that the act of Going for Refuge was the central and definitive act of the Buddhist life and that becoming a monk (including formal Going Forth) was of spiritual significance and value only to the extent that it was an actual expression of one's Going for Refuge.

This is not to say that the formal taking of the Three Refuges did not feature prominently in the ordination ceremony. It featured very prominently indeed, but in such a way that its real significance tended to be obscured rather than revealed. Taking the Three Refuges (and Ten Sramanera Precepts) was simply one of the things one did when one became a novice monk. It was not seen as constituting the very essence of true monkhood, in comparison with which such things as shaving hair and beard, donning saffron robes of the prescribed cut, exhibiting the alms bowl (as well as the belt, water-strainer, needle and razor), saluting the feet of the preceptor, having one's own feet saluted by the laity, and sharing in the ceremonial food-offering were, in themselves,

Worthless as withered weeds,
Or idlest foam amid the boundless main.

Thus while U Chandramani was much concerned that I should pronounce the words of the Refuge-going formula with perfect correctness, both in Pali and in Sanskrit, and took a great deal of trouble to ensure this, he had absolutely nothing to say about the *meaning* of those words or about the significance of the act of Going for Refuge itself, so that in one respect, at least, I was no wiser after my sramanera ordination than I had been after taking Pansil from U Thittila. At our first meeting U Chandramani had, however, been gratified to learn that I had not only taken Pansil five years earlier but taken it from a *Burmese* monk, and this fact probably had something to do with his deciding to grant our – or at least my – request for ordination. Be that as it may, even though I had not yet realized the position Going for Refuge occupied in the Buddhist life – or rather, had not yet realized that being a Buddhist and Going for Refuge were in fact one and the same thing – I was conscious that between my taking Pansil in London and my becoming a monk in Kusinara there was a definite continuity, a continuity that had less to do with the nationality of my two preceptors than with the Three Jewels or Three Refuges themselves.

Since I have emphasized the lack of clarity with which I took sramanera ordination, I would not like to conclude this section without redressing the balance a little and emphasizing what an extremely positive occasion the ordination was for me. I felt delighted, thrilled, exhilarated and inspired, as well as intensely grateful for all the kindness I had received at the hands of U Chandramani and his little band of followers. Like my taking Pansil and my Going Forth, my sramanera ordination was not just part of a process, but was of value and significance on its own account.

6
Bhikshu Ordination

In many parts of the Buddhist world bhikshu ordination follows directly after sramanera ordination, provided the candidate is twenty or more years of age. In my own case a year and a half elapsed before I could take higher ordination, as it was also called, the principal reason for the delay being that in a non-Buddhist country like India it was no easy matter to bring together the minimum of ten bhikshus needed for the correct performance of the ceremony. Usually they could be brought together only on the occasion of major festivals, when bhikshus from many parts of the Buddhist world would be among the thousands of pilgrims flocking to the sacred places of north-east India. Thus it was that I received my bhikshu ordination at Sarnath on 24 November 1950 (a full moon day), on the occasion of the nineteenth anniversary of the opening of the Mulagandhakuti Vihara, having come down from Kalimpong for the purpose.

The ceremony took place in the Burmese temple, in the presence of four or five dozen people, and lasted about an hour. U Chandramani being unavoidably absent, his place as preceptor (*upadhyaya*) was taken by a well-known preacher from Rangoon, so that my bhikshu ordination, like my taking Pansil and my sramanera ordination, took place under the auspices of the Burmese branch of the Theravada Monastic Order. Since I have given a fairly detailed account of the ceremony in the as yet unfinished continuation of *The Thousand-Petalled Lotus*, in this paper I shall mention only those aspects of it that are relevant within the present context, that is, the tracing of the history of my Going for Refuge. What struck me most forcibly, both at the time and afterwards, was the fact that nowhere in the ceremony was there any provision for Going for Refuge, in the sense of repeating the Refuge-going formula after the preceptor. True, I had to repeat it after my teacher (*acarya*) as part of the re-ordination as a sramanera which, in accordance with tradition, preceded my ordination as a bhikshu, but in the bhikshu ordination ceremony itself Going for Refuge did not feature in any way, nor was it so much as mentioned afterwards. This was all the more remarkable in that – as I discovered only much later – bhikshu ordination had in the early days of Buddhism consisted simply in the threefold repetition of the Refuge-going formula. Mention was, however, made of the four reliances (*nissaya*) of the monk, which my preceptor in fact explained to me after the ceremony proper. Ideally a monk should rely on alms for food, on dust-heap rags for robes, on the roots of trees for lodging, and on cow's urine for medicine; but should he find this too difficult he might accept invitations to meals, wear robes made of various materials, live in a house or cave, and take ghee, butter, oil, honey, and sugar when sick. Thus full allowance was made for human weakness, though I could not help wondering whether a monk would not be more likely to adhere to the four reliances if he was not given the impression, so soon after his ordination, that he was not really expected to take them seriously.

During the ordination itself, however, I was troubled by no such doubts or reservations. Indeed, I was troubled by very few thoughts of any kind, the reason for this being that proceedings were for the most part conducted in 'Burmese Pali', so that for much of the time I was free simply to immerse myself in the positive atmosphere generated by the occasion. With me in the consecrated area, and completely surrounding me, were monks of four different nationalities, including the same Maha Bodhi Society bhikshus who had turned down my request for ordination eighteen months earlier. Surrounding the monks, but outside the consecrated area, were laymen and laywomen of at least six different nationalities, while immediately behind the monks and in front of the laity was a Tibetan Incarnate Lama, who, since he was an upholder of the Bodhisattva ideal, could be regarded as transcending the dichotomy between monk and layman. It was therefore not surprising that despite the lack of provision for Going for Refuge – indeed, despite my own lack of clarity on this all-important subject – I should have been conscious of the third Jewel, at least, in a way that I had not been conscious of it before. Whether this consciousness amounted to Going for Refuge to the Spiritual Community in the strict sense is doubtful, but at least it gave me my first intimation of what such Going for Refuge was really like.

7
'Taking Refuge in the Buddha'

In the introduction to this paper I spoke of the 'Chinese' poems I wrote at Quartermaine shortly after the first ordinations into the Western Buddhist Order (Triratna Buddhist Community). These were by no means my first poems, nor were they to be my last. I have in fact been writing poetry, of a sort, since I was eleven or twelve and probably have not finished writing it even yet. Quite a few of my poems give expression to thoughts and feelings that, for one reason or another, could find an outlet in no other way. Thus whatever their deficiencies as poetry, they may be of interest and value as an indication of my state of mind at the time of writing. As I have commented in the preface to *The Enchanted Heart*, with regard to the poems selected from my poetic output for the years 1946-1976 for inclusion in that volume:

> Many of them, if not the majority, have only a biographical – even a sentimental – interest. They give expression to passing moods and fancies as well as to deeper experiences and insights. They also reflect my responses to my

surroundings. As such they constitute a sort of spiritual autobiography, sketchy indeed, but perhaps revealing, or at least suggesting, aspects of my life that may not otherwise be known.

This is certainly true of a poem entitled 'Taking Refuge in the Buddha', which I wrote when I had been a bhikshu for just over two years. The poem was written in Kalimpong, where for the last three years I had been doing my best to obey my teacher Kashyapji's injunction to 'stay there and work for the good of Buddhism'. Neither in my work for Buddhism nor in my personal life had I received the help and cooperation to which, I felt, I was entitled, and the poem gave expression to my deep disappointment and frustration. The circumstances that led to its production are briefly described in the diary I was then keeping. The entry for Monday 26 January reads: 'Puja and meditation. The remarks Joe made yesterday caused me to feel that I had no earthly refuge, that none understood me or sympathized with the aim I was striving to achieve. In this mood a line which I had composed some months ago as the refrain of a poem came into my mind, and during breakfast I composed the first one and a half verses of "Taking Refuge in the Buddha". Then came Sachin, and we read seven of Shakespeare's Sonnets, and studied a Chapter of Logic, on which I dictated him seven pages of notes.

After he had gone I completed the poem.' The 'Joe' referred to in this extract was an elderly and extremely cantankerous Canadian Buddhist who had settled in Kalimpong with the intention of helping me in my work; 'Sachin' was a talented Nepalese college student to whom I gave tuition in English and Logic, and for whose benefit I subsequently wrote my essay 'Advice to a Young Poet'.

'Taking Refuge in the Buddha' is too long to be quoted in full, but its seven eight-line stanzas constituted a resounding declaration of my heartfelt conviction that for me there could be no refuge in the beauties of nature, no refuge in the world of literature and the arts, no refuge in politics, no refuge in professional or commercial activity, no refuge in Christianity, Islam, or Hinduism, no refuge in the observances of conventional Buddhism, no refuge anywhere in conditioned existence, and no refuge, even, in a nirvana conceived simply as the opposite of samsara. For me there could be refuge only at the feet of the Buddha, above the dualism of subject and object. The fact that in this poem I spoke only of taking Refuge in the Buddha did not, of course, mean that I did not likewise take Refuge in the Dharma and the Sangha; it simply meant that my taking Refuge in the Dharma and the Sangha was contained within my taking Refuge in the Buddha, even as the Dharma-Jewel and the Sangha-Jewel were themselves contained within the Buddha-Jewel.

As Gampopa points out in his *Jewel Ornament of Liberation*, the English translation of which I read eagerly on its appearance five years later, the ultimate refuge is the Buddha alone. 'He is the ultimate refuge because he possesses the Dharmakaya and the devotees of the three paths, i.e. the path of the Sravakas, the Pratyekabuddhas, and the Bodhisattvas also find their fulfilment in him by obtaining the final pure Dharmakaya.' If one asks whether the Dharma and the Sangha are not the ultimate refuge the answer is in the negative for, as Gampopa goes on to explain, basing himself on the *Mahayana-uttaratantra*: 'The Dharma that is taught is only a collection of words and letters and has to be discarded like a raft when we have reached the other shore. The Dharma that is understood has two aspects, the Truth of the Path and the Truth of the Cessation of Misery. The former is a product and not eternal, hence is deceptive and no refuge, while the latter has no real existence being compared by the Sravakas to the extinction of a lamp. The Sangha itself also has taken Refuge in the Buddha, because it was afraid of Samsara and so is no ultimate refuge.' In short, 'refuge is only one, the means is threefold', the Refuges having been split up into three simply as a way of attracting people of different spiritual capacities. Thus, even though I did not know it at the time, the conviction to which 'Taking Refuge in the Buddha' gave expression – the conviction, namely, that for me there could be

Refuge only in the Buddha – was fully in accordance with the best Buddhist tradition.

When I came to transcribe the poem into my 'poetry notebook' I placed at its head, by way of a motto, the words *Natthi me saranam annam, Buddho me saranam varam*, 'For me there is no other refuge, the Buddha is the supreme refuge.' These words were a quotation from the Tiratana Vandana or 'Salutation to the Three Jewels', which I had recited as part of my daily office ever since becoming a sramanera. Shortly after my bhikshu ordination I had, in fact, rendered the Vandana itself into English verse:

> *To all the Buddhas* [or Dharmas, or Sanghas] *of
>   the past,*
> *To all the Buddhas yet to be,*
> *And all the Buddhas that now are,*
> *My worship flows unceasingly.*
> *No other refuge than the Wake* [or the Law, or the
>   Brotherhood] –
> *Refuge Supreme – there is for me!*
> *Oh by the virtue of this truth*
> *May grace abound, and victory!*

Though I recited the Vandana in Pali and not in English the words 'Oh by the virtue of this truth / May grace abound, and victory!' haunted me in a way that the corresponding words in Pali never did. With their distant echoes of Bunyan, and still more distant echoes of St Paul, the words 'May grace abound, and victory!' were not quite a literal translation of the words *Hotu me jayamangalam*, but I thought they captured their spirit very well indeed. Whether or not this was the case, there is no doubt that the fact that I was reciting the Tiratana Vandana every day, and repeating 'May grace abound, and victory!' under my breath on all sorts of occasions, contributed to the growth of the feeling and the conviction which, at a time of disappointment and frustration, found expression in 'Taking Refuge in the Buddha.'

8

A Survey of Buddhism

A Survey of Buddhism was written between the end of 1954 and the beginning of 1956, on the basis of lectures delivered in Bangalore in the summer of 1954, and was published in 1957. It is sometimes referred to as my *magnum opus*, and such indeed it is in the sense that it is the most comprehensive and systematic of all my writings on Buddhism. It is, however, quite an early work. When I gave the lectures on which it is based I had been a Buddhist for thirteen years and a monk for five and, as I wrote in the preface to the fifth edition of the *Survey*, the giving of the lectures, and the subsequent preparation of them for publication in book form, 'gave me the opportunity of standing back and taking a look at the great spiritual tradition to which I had committed myself, and of trying to sum up, for my own benefit as much as for that of other people, what I had learned about Buddhism in the course of my thirteen years as a Buddhist and how, at the end of that time, I saw the Buddha's Teaching. It gave me the opportunity, in other words, of finding out what I really thought of Buddhism – what Buddhism really meant to me.'[3]

More than thirty years have passed. I have now been a Buddhist not for thirteen years but for forty-seven, and it would be strange if today I saw the Buddha's teaching in exactly the same way as I saw it then. It would be strange if there had been no change, or rather no development, in my thinking about Buddhism – strange if Buddhism did not mean even more to me now than it did when I wrote the *Survey*. This is not to say that I have found anything wrong with the fundamental principles on which the book is based, or any reason to change my approach to Buddhism or my method of treatment, even though the work admittedly has its limitations – limitations which I have tried to make good in some of my subsequent writings and lectures. Such changes as have taken place in my thinking about Buddhism during the last thirty years have taken place entirely as a result of the further application of some of the principles enunciated in the *Survey* itself. As I have explained in my preface to the fifth edition, in taking my look at Buddhism I was concerned principally to do two things. I was concerned to see Buddhism in its full *breadth* and in its ultimate *depth*, by which I meant that I was concerned firstly to see Buddhism as a whole, and secondly to see it in its deeper interconnections both within itself and in relation to the spiritual life of the individual Buddhist. Seeing Buddhism as a whole meant doing justice to all its principal teachings and major historical forms, as well as showing that these were interconnected by virtue of their common basic principles and their bearing on the spiritual life of the individual. Seeing it in its depth meant trying to understand why the Buddha had taught this or that doctrine, or what relation it had to the needs of the individual as he wrestled with the problems of existence.

Breadth and depth were, however, inseparable. As the years went by I increasingly found that the more I related Buddhism to the spiritual life of the individual Buddhist, the more I saw it in its deeper interconnections within itself, and the more I saw it in its deeper interconnections within itself the more I saw it not as a collection of miscellaneous parts but as an organic whole. This was nowhere more apparent than in the case of Going for Refuge, which I eventually came to see as the central and definitive act of the Buddhist life and as the unifying principle, therefore, of Buddhism itself. At the stage in the history of my Going for Refuge which we have now reached – the stage represented by *A Survey of Buddhism* – I did not, however, realize the absolute centrality of the act of Going for Refuge, or rather, though I realized it in principle to some extent, I had not yet worked out its implications, which were in fact very far-reaching indeed.

If the index to the sixth edition of the *Survey* can be relied on, in the body of the work (as distinct from the Introduction, which was added later) the

Three Jewels are mentioned as a triad three times and the Three Refuges once, while Going for Refuge is mentioned six times. Interestingly enough, the most extended treatment of the subject is to be found in chapter IV, 'The Bodhisattva Ideal', in the section dealing with the preliminary devotional practices undertaken by the would-be Bodhisattva. These preliminary devotional practices are collectively known as Supreme Worship (*anuttara-puja*) or – as we generally say in the Triratna Buddhist Community – the Sevenfold Puja, the third 'practice' (or the second, if one follows Shantideva in conflating the first and second practices and counting six altogether instead of seven) being that of Going for Refuge (*sarana-gamana*). The key passage in the two pages dealing with Going for Refuge as one of the preliminary devotional practices occurs at the very beginning, and reads as follows:

> Going for Refuge (*sarana-gamana*) means, of course, Going for Refuge to the Buddha, the Dharma, and the Sangha. While even a non-Buddhist can, in a sense, respect and honour the Triple Gem, to take Refuge in them is the prerogative of the professing and practising Buddhist alone. Formal Refuge, which is held to constitute one a member of the Buddhist community, can be taken simply by repeating after any ordained monk

the Refuge-formula and the Five Precepts. But effective Refuge, of which the formal Refuge is at once the expression and the symbol, can be taken only by one who has an understanding of the true nature of the Triple Gem. The deeper this understanding goes, the more effective will be his Refuge. Taking Refuge in the Triple Gem is not, therefore, an act to be done once and for all time, but something which grows with one's understanding of Buddhism. The Refuge is complete when one's understanding of Buddhism is complete, that is to say, when one attains Enlightenment. Then, paradoxically enough, there is no Going for Refuge: the Enlightened One is his own Refuge.[4]

I then go on to discuss the minimum degree of understanding needed for taking effective Refuge in the Three Jewels, and in this connection point out that, inasmuch as the Mahayana has a deeper understanding of the Triple Gem than the Hinayana, the significance which it attaches to the act of taking Refuge is naturally more profound. Nevertheless, I am at pains to make it clear that, doctrinal differences notwithstanding, 'all schools of Buddhism, whether of the Great or Little Vehicle, agree in recognizing the decisive importance in the Buddhist life of the act of taking Refuge' – a statement which to some extent anticipates my present general position. In the 'key passage' itself I distinguish between formal Refuge and effective Refuge in much the same way that I was later to distinguish between provisional (or ethnic) Refuge, and between effective Refuge and real Refuge. More important still, I insist that taking Refuge in the Triple Gem is not an act to be done once and for all time but something that grows with one's understanding of Buddhism – an insight that made the development of my thinking about Buddhism possible and which underlies much of my current thinking, except that I would now add that one's understanding of Buddhism grows as one's Going for Refuge becomes more effective and more real.

Yet despite such anticipations and semi-anticipations the key passage in my discussion of Going for Refuge, considered as one of the preliminary devotional practices undertaken by the would-be Bodhisattva, cannot really be regarded as foreshadowing either the deeper understanding of the significance of the act of Going for Refuge at which I eventually arrived, or my realization of the implications of that act, properly understood, for the whole theory and practice of Buddhism. I am not referring to the comparatively unimportant fact that, speaking of formal Refuge in the Triple Gem, I say that it can be taken 'simply by repeating after any ordained monk the Refuge-formula and the Five Precepts.'

This statement is in any case modified towards the end of my discussion of Going for Refuge as one of the preliminary devotional practices of the would-be Bodhisattva, where I say that the Refuges are 'generally taken from a bhikshu' and that, in the absence of a bhikshu, 'a Buddhist assembly may be "led" in the taking of the Three Refuges by any senior lay devotee' – though even this does not go nearly far enough, and begs all sorts of questions. In insisting that the key passage in the *Survey's* most extended treatment of Going for Refuge cannot really be regarded as foreshadowing my later views on the subject, I am referring to something much more subtle and profound. Though in the purely formal or abstract sense my understanding of the meaning of Going for Refuge was not incorrect, and though I even realized in principle, to some extent, the absolute centrality of the act of Going for Refuge, I did not actually place that act, as I then understood it, at the very heart and centre of Buddhism, with all the momentous consequences that would have then followed. I did not accord it that absolute priority over all other acts which, by its very nature, it demands.

Thus at the beginning of the 'key passage' already quoted, after defining 'Going for Refuge' as Going for Refuge to the Buddha, the Dharma, and the Sangha, I continue: 'While even a non-Buddhist can, in a sense, respect and honour the Triple Gem, to take

43

Refuge in them is the prerogative of the professing and practising Buddhist alone.' This is really to put the cart before the horse, for, as I observed in section 4 in connection with my Going Forth, one does not Go for Refuge because one is a Buddhist but is a Buddhist because one Goes for Refuge. Similarly, Going for Refuge is not simply one of the preliminary devotional practices which one undertakes in order to develop the Bodhicitta or 'Will to Enlightenment', thus becoming a Bodhisattva – it is *because* one Goes for Refuge that one is a Bodhisattva. As I came to realize only at a subsequent stage in the history of my Going for Refuge, the Bodhisattva's aspiration to attain Supreme Enlightenment for the benefit of all sentient beings is in fact the altruistic dimension of the act of Going for Refuge itself, which by its very nature cannot be regarded as having implications for oneself alone. Provisional Going for Refuge can, of course, be regarded as a means to the arising of the real Bodhicitta; but equally, the provisional Bodhicitta can be regarded as a means to real Going for Refuge. We must be careful not to make the mistake of thinking that what is, in fact, only a 'revised version' of a certain stage of spiritual development is actually a higher stage.

The Mahayana came to see the (real) Bodhicitta as superior to the (provisional) Going for Refuge for much the same reason that it came to see the Bodhisattva ideal as superior to the Arhant ideal, i.e.

because in the hands of the Hinayana the concept of Going for Refuge had lost much of its original significance, so that a fresh formulation of what it had been intended to convey had to be found. Earlier on in chapter IV, 'The Bodhisattva Ideal', in the section entitled 'The Unifying Factor', I describe the Bodhisattva ideal as 'the principal unifying factor' not only for the Mahayana schools but for the entire Buddhist tradition. But inasmuch as the Bodhisattva is one in whom the Bodhicitta has arisen, and inasmuch as the arising of the Bodhicitta is the altruistic dimension of Going for Refuge, it is in fact the act of Going for Refuge that is the principal unifying factor in Buddhism. What I say about the Bodhisattva ideal in chapter IV of the *Survey* has to be read, where necessary, in the light of this realization.

In much the same way, those passages in chapters I–III of the *Survey* which intend to identify the Sangha or Spiritual Community with the Monastic Order must be read in the light of the realization that, as I have explained in section 5 of this paper, becoming a monk is of significance and value only to the extent that it is an expression of one's Going for Refuge. Indeed, in chapter II of the *Survey*, 'Hinayana and Mahayana', in the section entitled 'What is Mahayana Buddhism?', having commented on the Mahayana bhikshus' healthier and more truly orthodox attitude to the formal aspects of monasticism, I not only point out that, once it has been admitted that a Bodhisattva may be either a monk or a layman, 'it becomes impossible to identify the spiritual life exclusively with a life of monasticism', but also make it clear that the Buddha himself did not identify commitment to the spiritual life with adoption of the monastic lifestyle, by quoting *Dhammapada* verse 142 to this effect.[5]

In this connection I have one more point to make before concluding this section. In various parts of the *Survey*, but particularly in chapter II, section 4, 'Factors in the Emergence of the Mahayana', I severely criticize the Hinayana in general and the Theravada Sangha (i.e. the Theravada Monastic Order) in particular for what I term 'over-attachment to the merely formal aspects of monasticism', which I in fact enumerate as one of the five factors which were responsible, on the negative side, for the emergence of the Mahayana as a historical phenomenon. Re-reading my strictures twenty-one years later I found them milder than I had thought and, though severe enough, fully justified, and therefore wrote in the preface to the fifth (1980) edition of the *Survey*: 'In the light of subsequent experience I am convinced that my criticisms of the modern Theravada were – and still are – not only fully justified but absolutely necessary, and I do not retract a word of what I wrote. I would only like to add that, far from being confined to the modern Theravada, the canker of

46

formalism can sometimes be found in other forms of Buddhism too, not least in contemporary Zen.'[6] Ten years further on I would like to add that although my criticisms of the Theravada were 'harsh' (as one of my friends called them), and although that 'harshness' was fully justified, they were in reality not harsh enough, in the sense that they were not sufficiently radical. Though I speak in unfavourable terms of 'that identification of the religious life exclusively with the formal aspects of monasticism which is so prominent a feature of the Hinayana' I do so only incidentally, and in giving my various colourful examples of formalism and hypocrisy within the modern Theravada (Monastic) Sangha do not sufficiently bring out the fact that what is really wrong with it is its confusion of Going for Refuge with becoming a monk – commitment with lifestyle. Members of the Theravada (Monastic) Sangha are not so much bad monks as bad Buddhists. Indeed, it is possible to be a good monk, in the formalistic sense, and at the same time a bad Buddhist. One might even go so far as to say that it is possible to be a bad monk and a good Buddhist.

If one bears this in mind, and bears in mind that the arising of the Bodhicitta or 'Will to Enlightenment' represents the altruistic dimension of Going for Refuge, one will have gone a long way towards placing the act of Going for Refuge at the very heart and centre of Buddhism, and a long way, therefore, towards seeing the extent to which my later thinking about Buddhism is implicit in my earlier.

9
Dhardo Rimpoche and
The Path of the Buddha

When I was in the midst of writing the *Survey* a Tibetan friend asked me to help him with the English of an article on 'Buddhism in Tibet' that he had agreed to write for an American publication. The friend was Lobsang Phuntsok Lhalungpa, an official of the Tibetan government who had grown up in Lhasa and now lived in Kalimpong, and the publication was *The Path of the Buddha*, a book aiming to present Buddhism 'from the Buddhist point of view'. Helping Lobsang with the English of his article actually involved the complete rewriting of some three-hundred foolscap pages of manuscript, my friend's command of the 'tongue / That Shakespeare spake' being then quite rudimentary. Though the work was onerous, and could hardly have come at a more inconvenient time, I did it willingly, the more especially when I discovered that in writing his article Lobsang Phuntsok was drawing not so much on his own knowledge of Tibetan Buddhism as on the knowledge of an eminent Incarnate Lama who after-

49

wards became one of my most revered teachers. This was Dhardo Rimpoche, the Greatly Precious One of Dharsendo.

For a period of several months, therefore, I not only carried on writing the *Survey* but wrestled with Lobsang Phuntsok's grammar and syntax, not to mention his spelling and handwriting. Sometimes what he had written was so confused as to be unintelligible. When that was the case I was obliged to call on him for verbal explanations of what he was trying to say, and these explanations often led to our becoming involved in prolonged doctrinal discussion. Such discussion did not always succeed in making his account of Shunyata, or of the Trikaya doctrine, seem any the less confused, with the result that he had to refer back to Dhardo Rimpoche, the original source of his material, for further clarification. Having done this, he could be sure that whatever explanations he now gave me were correct and I, for my part, could be sure that in rewriting his pages in accordance with them I was not misinterpreting Tibetan Buddhism. All this naturally took time, but eventually the work was done and the article despatched to the United States where, after being edited and drastically shortened, it appeared as chapter 6 of *The Path of the Buddha* in 1957.

As so often happens, a benefit conferred turned out to be a benefit received. As a result of rewriting Lobsang Phuntsok Lhalungpa's article, and especially as a result of the prolonged doctrinal discussion to which this frequently led, in the space of three or four months I received from him and, through him, from Dhardo Rimpoche, a comprehensive grounding in the history, the schools, the doctrines, and the practices of Tibetan Buddhism – a grounding that often went far beyond the topics actually dealt with in the article. At a time when reliable books on Tibetan Buddhism could be counted on the fingers of one hand the experience was of immense value to me, and laying down my pen after rewriting the last sentence of Lobsang's manuscript I felt as though I had been given an intensive course in the subject. Nevertheless, owing to my preoccupation with the writing of the *Survey* I was not in a position to absorb what I had learned to the extent that I might otherwise have done, though traces of my newly acquired knowledge of Tibetan Buddhism are discernible here and there in my *magnum opus*. Among the topics with regard to which I was unable to absorb what I had learnt was the topic of 'Going for Refuge', which was dealt with in a short section of the article entitled 'The Three Precious Ones' (i.e. the Three Jewels). According to Lobsang Phuntsok/ Dhardo Rimpoche, Tibetan Buddhists took heartfelt Refuge in the Buddha, the Dharma, and the Sangha, and this taking Refuge in the Triple Gem was 'the most fundamental belief and most widely accepted practice in Buddhism', preceding all other religious acts such as reading of scriptures, making of solemn vows, receiving ordination, performance of ceremonies, and practice of meditation.[7] Moreover, Tibetan Buddhists placed great emphasis on the good intention preceding the taking of the Three Refuges. 'The intention must be of a sincere and benevolent nature, supported by a strong resolve, and the vow itself [i.e. one's Going for Refuge] must be constantly borne in mind while performing any religious practices.'[8] Most important of all: 'The taking of the Three Refuges includes within its scope the taking of all the principles of Buddhism; one who does not take the Triple Gem is not a Buddhist.'[9]

The full significance of these statements, especially of the last, dawned on me only later, as I became more closely acquainted with the Tibetan Buddhist tradition through the study of books and through personal contact with Dhardo Rimpoche and other Incarnate Lamas. But before proceeding to deal with this stage in the history of my Going for Refuge, which in a sense constitutes a continuation of the stage dealt with in the present section, I must say something about my contact with Buddhists of a very different type – a contact which, in its own way, also contributed to the process whereby the meaning and significance of Going for Refuge became clear to me.

10

Ambedkar and the 'ex-Untouchables'

Bhimrao Ramji Ambedkar was an 'Untouchable'[10] from Bombay state who, overcoming enormous obstacles, became an economist, a lawyer, an educationalist, a politician and, finally, free India's first Law Minister and the chief architect of her Constitution. Throughout his life he fought for the amelioration of the lot of India's tens of millions of 'Untouchables' and for the removal of the age-old social, religious, economic, political, and educational disabilities imposed on them by the Caste Hindus – disabilities which reduced them to a state of virtual, even of actual, slavery. However, his efforts met with little or no success, and after thirty years of struggle Ambedkar came to the conclusion that the Caste Hindus were not going to mend their ways, that there was no salvation for the 'Untouchables' within Hinduism, and that they would have to change their religion. On 14 October 1956, when he had been out of office for six years, he therefore not only embraced Buddhism himself by publicly taking the Three Refuges and

Five Precepts from U Chandramani Maha Thera, from whom I had received my sramanera ordination, but also inaugurated the historic movement of mass conversion to Buddhism by administering those same Refuges and Precepts, together with twenty-two vows of his own devising, to the 380,000 'Untouchable' men, women, and children who had assembled for the occasion. Six weeks later he died.

As related in *Ambedkar and Buddhism*, I had known Ambedkar since 1952, when we met after an earlier exchange of letters, and during the critical period immediately following his death I did whatever I could to ensure that the movement of mass conversion to Buddhism continued. This involved the making of a whole series of lecture tours in the course of which I visited cities, towns, and villages all over central and western India and came into contact with tens upon tens of thousands of 'ex-Untouchable' Buddhists, some of whom I indeed received into Buddhism myself. But whether received into Buddhism by me, by a fellow monk, or by one of their own leaders, like their great emancipator they all became Buddhists simply by taking the Three Refuges and Five Precepts. Taking the Refuges and Precepts by reciting them after a monk or other leading Buddhist was, of course, a standard procedure among lay Buddhists, especially in South East Asia. I had witnessed the ceremony at centres of the Maha Bodhi Society and elsewhere on numerous occasions, and had myself conducted it scores of times. But never before had I seen the Three Refuges and Five Precepts taken with the sincerity, zeal, and fervour that I saw them taken by the largely illiterate and wretchedly poor 'ex-Untouchables', many of whom had travelled a hundred miles or more on foot for the purpose. For the 'born Buddhists' of Ceylon and Burma, 'taking Pansil', as the Sinhalese called it, was little more than a pious formality, the sort of thing that a good Buddhist did, and not so much an expression of commitment to the Three Jewels as an affirmation of one's cultural and ethic identity. In the case of the 'ex-Untouchables' it was very different. For them taking the Refuges and Precepts, or becoming Buddhists, meant conversion in the true sense of the term. It meant not only the repudiation of Hinduism, not only deliverance from what Ambedkar called 'the hell of caste', but also being spiritually reborn in the sense of becoming free to develop in every aspect of their lives, whether social, economic, cultural, or religious. Indeed, as I could see from the light in their eyes and the rapturous look on their faces, in repeating the words of the ancient Pali formula the 'ex-Untouchables', far from just 'taking Pansil', were in fact giving expression to their heart-felt conviction that Buddhism was their only hope, their only salvation. They were Going for Refuge to the Three Jewels.

In the course of my tours I had many opportunities of seeing Ambedkar's followers take the Three

Refuges and Five Precepts, sometimes in very large numbers, and the sight of their sincerity, zeal, and fervour never failed to move me deeply. Moreover, I felt that they were taking the Refuges and Precepts, and becoming Buddhists, out of feelings very similar to those which, in my own case, had found an outlet in the poem 'Taking Refuge in the Buddha'. There was one big difference. Whereas I had written my poem after a single experience of disappointment and frustration, they had all gone for Refuge as a result of a lifetime of systematic harassment and humiliation. But though the difference was a big one, it was quantitive rather than qualitative, so to speak, and in spite of it I felt very close to my 'ex-Untouchable' brothers and sisters. It did not matter that I was English and they were Indian, or that I was a monk and they were laymen and laywomen. For them, as for me, there could be Refuge only at the feet of the Buddha, even though their conception of that Refuge was less metaphysical than mine.

Thus as a result of my contact with the 'ex-Untouchable' Buddhists I came closer to seeing that monasticism and the spiritual life were not identical, and that Going for Refuge was the principal unifying factor in Buddhism. I came closer to seeing that Going for Refuge was the central and definitive act of the Buddhist life.

11

More Light from
Tibetan Buddhism

The English Translation of Gampopa's *Jewel Ornament of Liberation* appeared in 1959, by which time my personal contact with Dhardo Rimpoche had deepened and I had received Tantric initiation from Jamyang Khyentse Rimpoche. As Dr Herbert V. Guenther, the scholarly translator of the work, explained in his preface:

> The work belongs to the group of texts which are known as 'Stages on the Path' (*lam.rim*). They are manuals that guide the student from the elementary tenets of Buddhism to the profoundest realization of Buddhahood. sGam.po.pa's work seems to have been the first Tibetan text of this kind and it has remained famous to the present day. It deals with the whole of Buddhism in such a lucid manner that it can be studied and understood without constantly looking up long-winded and often rather obscure commentaries and

sub-commentaries. It is therefore a real 'Jewel Ornament', a title that is an allusion to a particular type of literature known as 'adornments' (*alankara*) in Buddhist Sanskrit, because they give the choicest and most important subjects in a highly polished and rather concise form. Another outstanding feature of sGam.po.pa's work is that it is addressed to all people who are, or may become, spiritually inclined. It appeals to the layman as well as the monk and the philosopher who unceasingly pursues man's perennial quest for the meaning of life.[11]

On going through the work thus described I found it to consist of twenty-one chapters, one of which was headed 'Taking Refuge'. Though the manner in which Gampopa dealt with this supremely important step was certainly lucid, the fact that he explained it by way of 'nine topics of taking Refuge', most of which were divided and subdivided and even sub-sub-subdivided, gave his whole treatment of Going for Refuge an air of pedantry and scholasticism that was hardly in keeping with the spirit of the subject. This did not bother me, however, though it has bothered others ('laymen' studying the *Jewel Ornament* have found it less appealing than Guenther thought they would, mainly on account of its scholasticism), and when I read Gampopa's chapter on 'Taking Refuge' for the first time it was with a sense of light being shed upon the topic. Besides pointing out that the Buddha was the only Refuge, as I mentioned in section 7 in connection with my poem, he explained why powerful deities like Brahma, Vishnu, and Mahadeva are unable to provide us with a refuge, singled out 'not hurting other beings' as the consequence of taking Refuge in the noble Dharma, distinguished between the different levels of taking Refuge even more radically than I had done in the *Survey*, enumerated the eight benefits of taking Refuge, and made it clear that the difference between the Pratimoksa and the Bodhisattva-discipline was primarily one of attitude. But what really shed light on the topic of Going for Refuge was the fact that Gampopa had devoted a whole chapter to it. The medium was the message, the message being that 'Taking Refuge' (as Guenther unfortunately called it) was not just a formality, not something one did to show that one was a Buddhist, but actually one of the stages of the spiritual path – the *Jewel Ornament* itself being a guide to the Path, as Guenther had explained in his preface.

But though light was shed on Going for Refuge both by Gampopa's treatment of the topic and by the fact that he had devoted a whole chapter of his book to it, that light was by no means sufficient to illuminate the subject completely. For Gampopa the Hinayana represented a lower and the Mahayana a higher stage of the Path, and since Going for Refuge epitomized the Hinayana, just as the arising of the Bodhicitta or

Will to Enlightenment epitomized the Mahayana, it was in effect the arising of the Bodhicitta that was the central and definitive act of the (Mahayana) Buddhist life, rather than Going for Refuge. Going for Refuge, together with the observance of the Pratimoksa, was a means to the arising of the Bodhicitta, just as the Bodhicitta itself was a means of entering upon the Vajrayana through the receiving of abhishekha or 'Tantric initiation'. In Gampopa's own words, those taking Refuge in the Three Jewels were the 'working basis' for the arising, or as Guenther called it the development, of the Bodhicitta.

The reason why Gampopa was unable to see the Bodhicitta as the altruistic dimension of Going for Refuge was, of course, his lack of a sufficiently broad historical perspective. For him, both the Hinayana and the Mahayana had been taught by the Buddha. He was therefore unable to see them as representing successive developments from the Buddha's Original Teaching, and because he was unable to see them in this way he was unable to appreciate (1) that historically speaking the Mahayana was to a great extent a restatement of the Original Teaching in terms more in accordance with the spirit, as distinct from the letter, of that Teaching than were those of the Hinayana, and (2) that in the Mahayana restatement of the Original Teaching the place of Going for Refuge was occupied by the arising of the Bodhicitta. Thus he had no alternative but to treat Going for Refuge as a means to the

arising of the Bodhicitta, which meant that Going for
Refuge was at least recognized as constituting a definite stage of the Path, as indeed it had been since the
time of Atisha, and as it was to continue to be right
down to the present day – not just in Gampopa's
own Kagyupa school but throughout the whole
Tibetan Buddhist tradition. Nor was that all. While
in theory Going for Refuge remained a means to the
arising of the Bodhicitta, in the course of centuries it
became, in the hands of certain teachers, something
very much more. It was transformed, in fact, into a
virtually independent spiritual practice wherein the
entire personality of the practitioner was involved in
a particularly moving and significant manner, and
it was the discovery of this practice that, some three
years after the appearance of the English translation
of Gampopa's *Jewel Ornament of Liberation*, provided
me with further illumination on the topic of Going
for Refuge.

The discovery in question took place in Kalimpong,
shortly after I had received the abhishekha of the
Greatly Precious Guru, Padmasambhava, from
Khachu Rimpoche, a leading disciple of Jamyang
Khyentse Rimpoche. I received the abhishekha on 21
October 1962. The following morning I went into
town and on my way through the bazaar happened
to see a Tibetan monk squatting at the roadside. In
his lap was a small bundle of rather grubby xylograph
texts that he was offering for sale. Since the monk

was obviously in need of money, and since the texts were very cheap (so cheap that even I could afford to buy them), I at once bought them and returned with them to the Vihara, where I showed them to Khachu Rimpoche. His response was one of surprise and delight. They were *Nyingmapa* texts, he exclaimed joyfully, as he thumbed his way through them. Most of them had to do with the Greatly Precious Guru, and the fact that I had come across them so soon after receiving the abhishekha, and in such a totally unexpected manner, was extremely auspicious. It showed that I had a special connection with the Greatly Precious Guru, and with the Nyingmapa tradition, and that my efforts to realize the import of the teachings which the abhishekha had empowered me to practise would prove successful. Whether or not Khachu Rimpoche's 'reading of the signs' was correct is not for me to say. In any case, what I am concerned with at this juncture is the fact that among the texts I had bought, and which Khachu Rimpoche had greeted with such enthusiasm, was one entitled *Tharpe Delam* or 'The Easy Path to Emancipation'. This little work dealt with the general and special preliminaries to the practice of Ati Yoga, the highest teaching of the Nyingmapas, and the main general preliminaries consisted of the four mula or 'foundation' yogas, in the first of which Khachu Rimpoche had already given me some instruction. The first mula yoga was, of course, the Going for Refuge and Prostration practice, the remaining three being the Arising of the Bodhicitta, the Meditation and Mantra Recitation of Vajrasattva, and the Offering of the Mandala, after which followed the Guru Yoga. Having received further instruction from Khachu Rimpoche, I therefore took up the Going for Refuge and Prostration practice, as well as the other mula yogas, and continued to do it regularly until my departure for England two years later. With the help of Dhardo Rimpoche, I moreover made a rough translation of the entire *Tharpe Delam*. Though I was able to do the Going for Refuge and Prostration practice for only two years, which by Tibetan standards was not very long, during this period I had a more intense and more sustained experience of Going for Refuge than ever before. I also arrived at a clearer understanding of the fact that 'the taking of the Three Refuges includes within its scope the taking of all the principles of Buddhism', and a clearer understanding, therefore, of the meaning and value of the act of Going for Refuge itself.

Those members of the Order who have done the Going for Refuge and Prostration Practice will hardly need to be told why this should have been so. At the beginning of the practice one visualizes the Greatly Precious Guru, Padmasambhava, the founder and patron of the Nyingmapa tradition, seated on the calyx of a lotus which itself rests on a multi-coloured cloud floating in the midst of a brilliantly blue sky;

and one sees Padmasambhava as the embodiment of all the Buddhas. Below Padmasambhava, seated on the petals of the lotus, are one's various gurus, below them the four orders of Tantric divinities, and lower still the dharmapalas and dakinis. On the four sides of the lotus, i.e. the central lotus on the calyx of which sits Padmasambhava, are four more lotuses. On the front lotus stand Sakyamuni and the other human Buddhas; on the lotus to the right (i.e. to the right of Padmasambhava) the principal Bodhisattvas, and on the lotus to the left the leading Arhants, while on the rear lotus are piled the volumes of the sacred scriptures. In front of the Refuge Tree, as it is called, (for the five lotuses all spring from a single stem) is oneself, together with all sentient beings. Having visualized Padmasambhava and the other objects of Refuge in this way, one repeats not the usual Refuge-going formula but a slightly more elaborate 'Tantric' version, saying aloud 'OM AH HUM, to the best of all Refuges I go. To the Lama the Buddha, the Lama the Dharma, the Lama the Sangha; to the Lama the Sri Maha Heruka; to the Lama the All-Performing King; to the Three Jewels in one, Guru Rimpoche, for Refuge I go.' With each repetition one prostrates oneself before the visualized Refuge Tree (which one carries on visualizing throughout the session), or before its iconic counterpart. Thus in doing the Going for Refuge and Prostration Practice one Goes for Refuge with body, speech, and mind, that is, with the whole of one's being. One Goes for Refuge with one's mind by visualizing Padmasambhava and the other objects of Refuge on their respective lotuses, one Goes for Refuge with one's speech by repeating the words of the 'Tantric' Refuge-going formula, and one Goes for Refuge with one's body by making a full-length prostration. At the conclusion of the practice white light issues from the objects of Refuge and, falling upon oneself, one's father and all men, and one's mother and all women, takes away all their sins, which are dissolved into light. This light returns to the objects of Refuge, whereupon the gurus, devas, dharmapalas, and so on are dissolved into the body of Padmasambhava, and Padmasambhava himself into the Void.

As those who have done the Going for Refuge and Prostration Practice will be aware, in the course of each session of practice one not only visualizes the Refuge Tree throughout; one also repeats the words of the ('Tantric') Refuge-going formula, and prostrates oneself, as many times as one can, the sessions being kept up until such time as one has completed at least 100,000 repetitions and 100,000 prostrations, as some members of the Order have actually done. It is therefore not surprising that the practice should have a very powerful effect, even to the extent of bringing about a radical change in one's mental and spiritual outlook. Indeed, as the months and the years go by the practitioner may well find himself becoming so deeply absorbed in the experience of Going for Refuge that it is no longer possible for him to think of the Going for Refuge and Prostration Practice simply as one of the four mula yogas, or of the act of Going for Refuge itself simply as a means to the arising of the Bodhicitta. If he continues to think in such terms at all, he thinks of the Going for Refuge and Prostration Practice as being virtually a spiritual practice in its own right. Thus it may be said that the practice which I discovered shortly after receiving the abhishekha of the Greatly Precious Guru, and which provided me with further illumination on the topic of Going for Refuge, in fact represented a transposition of the act of Going for Refuge into the rich and colourful mode of the Indo-Tibetan Tantric tradition. As such, it also represented a restoration of Going for Refuge to something like its original place in Buddhism and in the Buddhist life.

But it was not only through Gampopa's *Jewel Ornament of Liberation* and my discovery of the Going for Refuge and Prostration Practice that light on the topic of Going for Refuge came to me from Tibetan Buddhism. Albeit less directly, light also came through personal contact with Tibetan Buddhists, especially through personal contact with certain eminent Nyingmapa Incarnate Lamas. Khachu Rimpoche, from whom I had received the Padmasambhava initiation, was a monk (as was Dhardo Rimpoche, who had been educated in the Gelugpa tradition); but other Nyingmapa Lamas were married. Indeed, among the married Lamas were some of the most eminent of all Nyingmapa Lamas – towering spiritual personalities whom Khachu Rimpoche himself regarded with the utmost veneration and from whom he was proud to receive initiation and instruction. As I came to know these Lamas myself I could not but recognize that in respect of learning and spiritual attainment there was, so far as I could see, no real difference between them and their celibate counterparts either in the Nyingmapa tradition itself or in the other Tibetan Buddhist traditions – though it could always be argued that had they not been married their spiritual attainment, at least, would have been even greater. Moreover, I could not but recognize that among the disciples by whom each of these Lamas was surrounded there existed a strong feeling of spiritual fellowship, and that in consequence of this feeling differences of lifestyle, particularly as between the monk and the lay disciples, were regarded as being of very little account. This gave me food for thought. Not all Buddhists, it seemed, identified the spiritual life with a life of strict monasticism in the way that the Theravadins of South East Asia did, or as some Gelugpas tended to do, despite the unifying influence of the Bodhisattva ideal. Thus my contact with the married Nyingmapa Lamas and their disciples had much the same result as my very different contact with the 'ex-Untouchable' Buddhists. I came closer to seeing that monasticism and the spiritual life were not identical, and closer, therefore, to realizing that what really mattered was not whether one was a monk or a layman, but the depth and intensity of one's Going for Refuge.

12

The Three Jewels and Other Writings

Between 1959 and 1964, when I returned to England, much of my time was devoted to literary work, and since it was during this same period that light on the topic of Going for Refuge came to me from Tibetan Buddhism it was only natural that a portion of that light should be reflected in some of the books and articles I was then engaged in producing.

The first of these, chronologically speaking, was an article on 'Ordination and Initiation in the Three Yanas' which appeared in the November 1959 issue of *The Middle Way*. As its title suggested, the purpose of the article was to clear up some of the confusion that, for many people, surrounded the whole subject of ordination and initiation, by explaining what the different ordinations and initiations actually were and how they corresponded to the three yanas and to the particular spiritual ideals in which those yanas found expression. The three yanas were, of course, the Hinayana, the Mahayana, and the Vajrayana, representing the three successive phases of development through which

Buddhism passed in India as well as the three progressive stages of spiritual ascent in the life of the individual Buddhist. But though Going for Refuge was mentioned in the article only once, in connection with ordination in the Hinayana, 'Ordination and Initiation in the Three Yanas' is far from being devoid of significance for the process whose history I am now tracing. Speaking of the difference between ordination or samvara on the one hand and (Tantric) initiation or abhishekha on the other, I pointed out that according to the fully developed Indo-Tibetan tradition the rite of admission to upasaka, sramanera, bhiksu, or Bodhisattva status is in each case termed a samvara, literally 'restraint', 'control', 'obligation', or 'vow'.[12] This was an important discovery. The fact that admission to upasaka, sramanera, bhikshu, and Bodhisattva status was in each case termed a samvara or 'ordination' meant that the differences between the various grades of religious persons were of far less significance than they were sometimes thought to be. In particular, it meant that the difference between the monk and the layman was not a difference between the ordained and the unordained. Both monks and laymen were ordained persons and both monks and laymen were, therefore, full members of the Buddhist spiritual community. This came very close to saying that samvara or ordination was a unifying rather than a dividing factor in Buddhism, and therefore very close to saying, as I afterwards did say, that ordination and Going for Refuge were in fact synonymous, and that Going for

Refuge was a unifying factor in Buddhism – indeed, that it was *the* unifying factor. Moreover, speaking of the three successive phases of Buddhist historical development, I pointed out that the Hinayana, Mahayana, and Vajrayana were not to be thought of as lying end to end, like so many sections of railway track, but that 'the earlier phase not only passes over into the latter, but is taken up into, and incorporated by it, and lives on in it.'[13] This meant, in effect, that Going for Refuge was taken up in the Bodhicitta, so that the way was now clear for my later realization that the Bodhicitta was the altruistic dimension of Going for Refuge.

In 1961, by way of contributing to the debate that followed the publication, in Ceylon, of the report of the Buddha Sasana Commission, I wrote an article to which I gave the controversial title 'Wanted: A New Type of Bhikkhu'. A year later, encouraged by the letters of appreciation I had received, I wrote a second article, to which I gave the hardly less controversial title 'Wanted: A New Type of Upasaka'. Both articles took the form of a series of aphorisms (54 in the case of the first article and 63 in the case of the second) and both were reproduced in virtually all the English language Buddhist journals. Since they were written mainly for a South East Asian Buddhist readership, the articles were reformist rather than revolutionary in tendency. As the concluding aphorism of the first article expressly stated, the 'new bhikkhu' was the old one adapted to modern conditions. Nevertheless, since both articles were concerned to stress the importance of moral and spiritual qualifications they both attempted, in effect, to bridge the gap between the monks and the laity. In the case of 'Wanted: A New Type of Bhikkhu' the attempt took the form of a strong attack on monastic formalism, which I continued to see as the besetting sin of the whole Theravada branch of the Monastic Order. 'The new type of bhikkhu will never commit the mistake of thinking that the wearing of the yellow robe makes him a monk', declared the opening aphorism, and in many of the succeeding aphorisms this principle was applied to specific areas of the monk's life. In the case of 'Wanted: A New Type of Upasaka' the attempt to bridge the gap between monks and laity took the form of a strong insistence that the upasaka, too, was a Buddhist and that it was incumbent on him to act accordingly. In the words of the first three aphorisms of the article: 'The new type of upasaka will never commit the mistake of thinking that it is really possible for anyone to be "a born Buddhist". He will not recite the Trisarana and Pancha Sila mechanically on Uposatha days without making any effort to embody them in his daily life. He will not think that the practice of the Dharma is the duty of the bhikkhu but not the upasaka.' Clearly my new type of bhikkhu and new type of upasaka would have a lot in common. So much in common would they have, indeed, that one might be forgiven for thinking that together they heralded the emergence of the Dharmachari (and Dharmacharini);

for, as I was shortly to realize, what Buddhists above all had in common – and what therefore constituted the fundamental basis of unity among them – was the fact that they all went for Refuge to the Buddha, Dharma, and Sangha, and that such Going for Refuge was of central importance in their lives.

As far as I know, this realization found its first unambiguous expression in the preface to *The Three Jewels*, where I spoke of Going for Refuge as 'the central act of the Buddhist life, from which all other [Buddhist] acts derive their significance, and without reference to which Buddhism itself is unintelligible.'[14] Since the preface is addressed from the Hampstead Buddhist Vihara, London, it must have been written in either 1965 or 1966, probably the latter. *The Three Jewels* itself, which was not published until 1967, had been written during the second half of 1961 and together with *The Eternal Legacy* constituted my major literary undertaking during the period covered by this section of my History. Like the latter work, it started life as a series of articles for *The Oriya Encyclopaedia* that, in the process of writing, considerably outgrew the purpose for which they had been commissioned. Though in it I did not speak of Going for Refuge in the terms in which, three or four years later, I spoke of it in the preface, some of my remarks on the subject of spiritual community showed how close I was to realizing the absolute centrality of that unique act both for the individual Buddhist and for Buddhism. Thus, having insisted that the true criterion of the relation between the Buddha and his followers was not physical, not spatio-temporal, but spiritual, and that we were nearest to him when we most perfectly followed his example, I went on:

> The Sangha is primarily the community of those who, by virtue of their immediate or remote approximation to Enlightenment, stand in spiritual relation to the Buddha and dwell spiritually in his presence. It is the community of those who, through their relationship with him, are also all spiritually related to one another.[15]

In other words, the Sangha is primarily the community of those who Go for Refuge, for it is Going for Refuge that enables us to achieve the stages of the Path and 'approximate' to Enlightenment, and Going for Refuge that forms the ultimate basis of our relationship with the Buddha and, therefore, the ultimate basis of our relationship with other members of the Sangha. Again, enlarging on the fact that in the broadest sense of the term the Sangha coincided with the entire Buddhist community, monastic and lay, male and female, I wrote:

> During the lifetime of the Master relations between the eremitical monks who had 'gone forth' and the householders at whose doors they daily stood for alms, and in whose outhouses and gardens they lodged during the rains, were

close and cordial, and a spirit of camaraderie prevailed. The latter could, if necessary, bring to the notice of the Master public complaints against the *parivrajakas*, and suggest changes in their mode of living. Such equalitarianism was natural. Their common devotion to the Buddha, and the extent to which his attainments transcended theirs, tended to reduce all distinctions among his followers, including that between monks and laymen, to a position of comparative insignificance. His impatience with the formalistic element in religion, and his uncompromising insistence on the necessity of personal realization of nirvana, moreover ensured that they should be distinguished, if at all, according to their intrinsic merits rather than their socio-ecclesiastical status. *'Even though a man be richly attired, if he develops tranquillity, is quiet, subdued and restrained, leading a holy life and abstaining from injury to all living beings – he is a* brahmana, *he is a* samana, *he is a* bhikkhu.*' That the homeless wandering monk, totally free from all worldly concerns, had a far better chance of reaching the Goal, was admitted, even emphasized; but that a householder, if sufficiently resolved, might sometimes reach it too, and that in the last resort it was transcendental attainment that mattered, not the wearing of yellow robes, more than one such saying of the Buddha testifies.[16]

Here the fact that it is their common devotion to the Buddha that tends to reduce all distinctions among his followers, including that between monks and laymen, to a position of comparative insignificance, implies that it is their common devotion to the Buddha that constitutes the fundamental basis of unity among Buddhists. But devotion to the Buddha finds its fulfilment in Going for Refuge to the Buddha, as well as to the Dharma and the Sangha. In saying that their common devotion to the Buddha tended to reduce all distinctions among his followers to comparative insignificance I was therefore, in effect, saying that it was their common Going for Refuge that constituted the fundamental basis of unity among them. Moreover, having referred to the schism that took place in the Buddhist community between one hundred and two hundred years after the Buddha's *parinirvana*, I pointed out that the Mahayana had 'evolved for all followers of the Buddha a common spiritual ideal', i.e. the Bodhisattva ideal, and worked out a common path, the Path of the Six (or Ten) Paramitas, thus lessening the tensions between the monastic and lay wings of the (Maha)sangha, 'which were now united through the pursuit of a common spiritual objective [i.e. Supreme Buddhahood] by means of the same, or similar, spiritual methods.' A common Vinaya for all Bodhisattvas, whether monks or laymen, was also evolved. Thus I had seen that the Mahayana had already made the Bodhisattva ideal the unifying factor of Buddhism, and having seen this I had only to realize

76

that the Bodhicitta was the altruistic dimension of Going for Refuge in order to see that it was in reality Going for Refuge that was the unifying factor and, therefore, 'the central act of the Buddhist life.'

'A bird's-eye view of Indian Buddhism', as I called it at one stage, was a lengthy article produced on the eve of my departure from India in 1964. Editorials for the *Maha Bodhi Journal* excepted, it was therefore the last of my writings to be produced during the period covered by the present section of this History. It had been commissioned by the Syndics of the Oxford University Press for the second edition of *The Legacy of India*, but having heard nothing from them for a long time and having assumed (wrongly, as it turned out) that they had decided not to use the article, in 1980 I included it in the fifth edition of *A Survey of Buddhism* as the Introduction to that work. Originally, very little of the light that had come to me from Tibetan Buddhism on the subject of Going for Refuge was reflected in its pages. Having dealt with the Arya Sangha and the Bhikshu Sangha or Order of Monks I wrote:

In a more general sense the Sangha comprises the entire Buddhist community, sanctified and unsanctified, the professional religieux and the lay devotees, men and women. As such it is sometimes known as the Mahasangha, or 'Great Assembly'. Lay devotees (*upasakas* and *upasikas*) are those who Go for Refuge to the

Three Jewels, worship the relics of the Buddha, observe the Five Precepts of ethical behaviour, and support the monks.

This did not go nearly far enough. In 1978, when revising the article for inclusion in the fifth edition of the *Survey*, I therefore made the following addition to the passage:

Although as time went on the life of the monks diverged more and more sharply from that of the laity the fact that all alike went for Refuge to the Buddha, the Dharma and the Sangha, remained a common, potentially uniting, factor – a factor that, in the case of the Mahayana, was strengthened by the development of the Bodhisattva ideal, which was an ideal equally for the monk and the layman, the nun and the laywoman.'[17]

This had the effect of bringing the article of 1964 more into line with my current thinking.

Mention of the preface to *The Three Jewels* and the inclusion of 'A bird's-eye view of Indian Buddhism' in the fifth edition of the *Survey* has, however, taken us rather too far ahead. Before leaving India I went through one more stage in the process by which the meaning, significance, and importance of Going for Refuge became clear to me.

13
Bodhisattva Ordination

The Bodhisattva ideal has attracted me from quite an early period of my Buddhist life. Indeed, it had attracted me from the time when, shortly after reading the *Diamond Sutra* and the *Sutra of Wei Lang*, I came across a copy of *The Two Buddhist Books in Mahayana*. The second of these books, which had been translated and compiled by Upasika Chihmann (Miss P.C. Lee of China), Bodhisattva in Precepts, was 'The Vows of the Bodhisattva Samantabhadra', which formed part of the *Avatamsaka* or *'Flower Ornament' Sutra*. This work I read repeatedly, and its picture of the infinitely wise and boundlessly compassionate Bodhisattva must have made a deep impression on me, for the words 'Thought succeeding thought without interruption, and in bodily, oral, and mental deeds without weariness'[18] kept going through my head for days together. It was as though they embodied Samantabhadra's – or any other Bodhisattva's – constant, unflagging fulfilment of his great vows through infinite time and infinite space. Seven or eight years later, shortly after my arrival in Kalimpong, I came across Shantideva's *Siksa-samuccaya* or 'Compendium of Instruction [for Novice Bodhisattvas]' and as a result was more strongly attracted to the Bodhisattva ideal than ever – so strongly, in fact, that attraction is far too weak a word for what I then felt. The truth was that I was thrilled, exhilarated, uplifted, and inspired by the Bodhisattva ideal, and my feeling for it found expression in some of the poems and articles I wrote during this period, as well as in chapter IV of *A Survey of Buddhism*. There were two reasons for my being so strongly affected. In the first place, there was the sheer unrivalled sublimity of the Bodhisattva ideal – the ideal of dedicating oneself, for innumerable lifetimes, to the attainment of Supreme Enlightenment for the benefit of all living beings. In the second, there was the fact that, as enjoined by my teacher Kashyapji, I was 'working for the good of Buddhism', and that I could not do this without strong spiritual support, the more especially since I received very little real help or cooperation from those who were supposedly working with me. This spiritual support I found in the Bodhisattva ideal, which provided me with an example, on the grandest possible scale, of what I was myself trying to do within my own infinitely smaller sphere and on an infinitely lower level.

It was therefore not surprising that on 12 October 1962 – nine days before receiving the Padmasambhava initiation – I should have received the Bodhisattva ordination. By that time I had been a Buddhist for more than twenty years, and a

monk for thirteen, and I had been working for the
good of Buddhism for twelve years. For the last five
years I had, indeed, been working for it not only
in Kalimpong and the neighbouring hill towns, as
originally enjoined, but among the 'ex-Untouchable'
Buddhists of central and western India. I therefore
felt ready to take the Bodhisattva ordination and, in
this way, give formal expression to my acceptance
of the Bodhisattva ideal. Moreover, I had found a
preceptor from whom I could take the ordination.
This was Dhardo Rimpoche, the Greatly Precious
One of Dharsendo, whom I had known since 1953
and whom I had come to revere as being himself a
living Bodhisattva. On the occasion of my sramanera
ordination U Chandramani had been concerned that
I should pronounce the words of the Refuge-going
formula correctly, but he had said nothing about the
meaning of those words or about the significance
of the act of Going for Refuge itself. Similarly, at
my bhikshu ordination my Burmese preceptor had
explained to me only the four reliances of the monk.
Dhardo Rimpoche, however, not only gave me the
Bodhisattva ordination but subsequently explained
the sixty-four Bodhisattva Precepts to me in consid-
erable detail, so that I was able to translate them
from Tibetan into English. What was no less important, whereas I had had no further contact with my
two previous preceptors after receiving ordination at
their hands, in the case of Dhardo Rimpoche I was

able to remain in regular personal contact with him for the rest of my stay in India.

But what effect did the taking of the Bodhisattva ordination have on me? At the time it gave me a definite sense of spiritual progression, for I still thought of the Hinayana, Mahayana, and Vajrayana as representing successive phases or stages of development and still, therefore, thought of the Bodhisattva ordination as being 'superior' to the bhikshu ordination, just as the bhikshu ordination was 'superior' to the upasaka ordination. In the long run, however, the taking of the Bodhisattva ordination had the effect of making me think of myself not as a monk who happened to accept the Bodhisattva ideal but rather as a (Triyana) Buddhist who happened to be a monk. Since the arising of the Bodhicitta – and becoming a Bodhisattva – was in fact the altruistic dimension of Going for Refuge, this in turn had the effect of making me think of myself simply as a monk who went for Refuge, or even as a human being who went for Refuge and who happened to live in monastic or semi-monastic fashion. Commitment was primary, lifestyle secondary.

14
Light from Vatican II

In August 1964, in response to an invitation from the English Sangha Trust, I returned to England and took up residence at the Hampstead Buddhist Vihara. My original intention was to stay for only four months, or at the most six, since I considered myself to be permanently domiciled in India; but in the end, after two years at the Hampstead Buddhist Vihara, I decided to stay in England indefinitely. I therefore paid a farewell visit to India and in March 1967 returned to England for good.

During the two years that I spent at the Hampstead Buddhist Vihara I was extremely busy, my time being occupied mainly with giving lectures and holding meditation classes, both at the Vihara itself and at the Buddhist Society, as well as with visiting the various provincial Buddhist groups. I was also available for personal interviews. Though there was no question of my being able to engage in literary work, I did however manage to find time for a certain amount of reading, being then particularly interested in informing myself about current developments in Christianity. One day I came across a book on the Second Vatican Council, and plunged into it immediately. Later I read other books on the subject with no less avidity. In one of these books the Roman Catholic Church was said to be characterized by authoritarianism, centralism, and triumphalism. Whether the characterization represented the Church's own verdict, via the Council, on its pre-conciliar Tridentine self, or whether it represented simply the verdict of the author, I do not remember, but it was a characterization that at once arrested my attention. I had heard of authoritarianism and centralism before, but I had not heard of triumphalism, which apparently meant exulting in the purely secular victories and achievements of the Church in general, and of the hierarchy and the clergy in particular, as though they were spiritual victories and spiritual achievements. In meant, in fact, mistaking the worldly power and glory of the Church for its spiritual power and glory, and thinking that in working for the former one was working for the latter.

This certainly shed light on the Roman Catholic Church, and explained much that was regrettable in the history of Christianity itself. But suddenly there struck me, with the force of a thunderbolt, the thought that the Theravada Monastic Order, too, was characterized by triumphalism. I recalled occasions on which Sinhalese monks had arrogantly insisted on taking precedence of everyone else and on being treated, in effect, like VIPs, in the belief that they were thereby upholding the supremacy of the Dharma. Similarly, I

LIGHT FROM VATICAN II

recalled the way in which visiting Thai bhikshus had confined themselves to teaching the newly converted 'ex-Untouchable' Buddhists such things as how to prostrate themselves before members of the Monastic Order and how to make offerings to them, as though in so doing they were propagating Buddhism among the 'ex-Untouchables' with a vengeance. In fact, the more I reflected on the insidious nature of triumphalism the more instances of it among Theravada monks I could recall, and the more instances I recalled, the more convinced I became that the Theravada Monastic Order was indeed characterized by triumphalism. Nor was that all. I had myself been ordained into the Theravada Monastic Order, and I realized with horror that I may well have been unconsciously influenced by its triumphalist attitude, if only to a limited extent. An element of triumphalism may even have crept into some of my writings, especially my editorials in the *Maha Bodhi Journal*. Having realized this, I resolved that in future I would be on my guard against triumphalism, both in myself and in others, and that I would discourage it by all possible means. Whether it characterized the Roman Catholic Church or not, there was no place for it in Buddhism and no place for it in the spiritual life.

Strange to say, at about the same time that I became aware that the Theravada Monastic Order was characterized by triumphalism I became more aware of the fact that there was a good deal of triumphalism in my immediate surroundings, as well as a good deal of formalism. Four or five Sinhalese and Thai monks were then staying with me at the Hampstead Buddhist Vihara, and all of them manifested a degree of triumphalism in their dealings with British Buddhists. So much was this the case, indeed, that I was reminded of the way in which the visiting Thai monks had taught the 'ex-Untouchable' Buddhists, for though the monks who were staying with me at the Vihara certainly did not confine themselves to teaching their British disciples how to prostrate themselves before members of the Monastic Order and how to make offerings to them, there was the same disproportionate emphasis on these things that I had witnessed in India. Such an emphasis was by no means a new thing to British Buddhists, however. Whether in the person of its Eastern or its Western representatives, the triumphalism of the Theravada Monastic Order had been a dominant factor in a section of the British Buddhist movement for more than a decade, as I quickly discovered when, a few days after my arrival in England, I shocked some participants in the Buddhist Society's annual summer school (and surprised and delighted others) by actually eating at the same table as everyone else. It was on account of incidents like this that I eventually concluded that, while there was a potential for the Dharma in the West, the existing British Buddhist movement had already strayed from the right path in certain respects, and a new Buddhist movement was badly needed.

15

'The Meaning of Conversion in Buddhism'

In the course of my two years at the Hampstead Buddhist Vihara I must have given upwards of two hundred lectures. Some of the people attending these lectures considered themselves to be Buddhists while others – no doubt the majority – did not. Among those who considered themselves Buddhists there were many who also considered themselves to have been converted to Buddhism, usually from Christianity, and this led to my giving more thought to what was meant by conversion, especially within the context of Buddhism, than I had done before. It also led to my delivering, under the title 'The Meaning of Conversion in Buddhism', a series of four lectures in which I dealt with conversion to (and within) Buddhism in terms of Going for Refuge, Stream Entry, the Arising of the Will to Enlightenment, and Turning About in the Deepest Seat of Consciousness.

These lectures were delivered in the summer of 1965, and in them I was able to give expression to some of the new ideas that had come to me as a result of my realization of the central importance of Going for Refuge in the Buddhist life. This is not to say that such ideas did not find their way into some of the other lectures I gave during my two years at the Hampstead Buddhist Vihara. Looking through my lecture notes of the period, in preparation for writing about this stage in the history of my Going for Refuge, I was indeed surprised at the extent to which later developments in my thinking had been anticipated. But though some of my new ideas (or rather, my new interpretations of old ideas) may have found their way into other lectures, it was only in the four lectures on 'The Meaning of Conversion in Buddhism' that certain of them found more or less systematic expression within the context of traditional Buddhist thought. Conversion itself I defined as a 'turning around' from a lower to a higher way of life or, more specifically, from a worldly life to a spiritual life. Sometimes it was a slow and gradual process, lasting many years; sometimes it was almost instantaneous, in which case one could speak of 'sudden conversion'. However it took place, it was of the greatest importance, as marking the beginning of the spiritual life, and hence was deserving of serious consideration. If the meaning of conversion was studied in connection with Buddhism, it would be found that it was not such a simple matter as had been supposed. In Buddhism conversion was of several kinds, and took place on different levels.

In terms of Going for Refuge, conversion meant the orientation of one's life in the direction of the Buddha, Dharma, and Sangha, which as 'the Three Jewels' represented the world of the highest spiritual values, or what was attractive and desirable above all else. It meant organizing one's life around the Three Jewels, and the greater part of the first lecture was devoted to an explanation of how this worked out in the case of each individual Jewel. In the case of the Buddha, Going for Refuge meant taking him as the living embodiment of the highest spiritual ideal. If anybody else was regarded as such there was no Refuge, and though one might be an admirer of the Buddha and Buddhism one would not be a Buddhist. This might seem narrow but was not really so. Devotion was by its very nature exclusive, for the heart could be fixed only on what was perceived as the highest. In the case of the Dharma, which was both 'teaching' and 'spiritual principle', Going for Refuge was of two kinds: intellectual and spiritual. Intellectually, it meant studying the doctrinal formulations in which the Dharma, as a spiritual principle, found expression; spiritually, it meant the personal realization of that principle. In the case of the Sangha, which at one and the same time denoted the spiritual hierarchy, the Monastic Order, and the whole Buddhist community, Going for Refuge was threefold in that one could Go for Refuge to the Sangha in all these senses. But there was a deeper meaning. Those who went for Refuge to the Sangha also went for Refuge to the Buddha and the Dharma, that is, they had a common spiritual teacher (or spiritual ideal) and a common teaching (or spiritual principle), and this tended to draw them together, even on the social plane. But what did one mean by 'together'? One did not mean physical proximity, or agreement on doctrinal questions, or even the attainment of the same stages of the spiritual path. It was rather more subtle than that. The 'together' lay in communication, which was not just an exchange of ideas but a vital mutual responsiveness, on the basis of a common spiritual ideal and a common spiritual principle. It was a common exploration, in complete harmony and complete honesty, of the spiritual world. In this way spiritual progress took place. The exploration might be between guru and disciple, or it might be between friends (this anticipated the 'vertical' and 'horizontal' communication/spiritual friendship of later expositions) – though in the course of communication such distinctions might have lost their significance. In any case, in Going for Refuge to the Sangha one would be Going for Refuge to spiritual communication from mere contact, which was in most cases meaningless and superficial.

In this way did I draw attention, in the first of my lectures on 'The Meaning of Conversion in Buddhism', to the fact that Sangha or spiritual community meant communication – a theme that, in later years, was to resound throughout the WBO and FWBO. Having done this, I reminded my listeners that Going for Refuge to the Three Jewels constituted conversion not merely in the sense of conversion from Christianity, or any other religion, to Buddhism, but in the sense of conversion from mundane life to spiritual life. It meant conversion from limited human ideals to an absolute spiritual ideal, from 'little systems' that 'have their day' to a path based on spiritual principles, and from meaningless worldly contact to meaningful spiritual communication. All this was involved when one repeated the words 'Buddham saranam gacchami', and so on. But even more than that, conversion meant 'changing into'. Going for Refuge was not just 'turning to' the Three Jewels but being transformed into them. Thus one aspect of the meaning of conversion in Buddhism was transformation into the Three Jewels. One's mind became Enlightened – became 'Buddha'; one's thoughts became in conformity with that Enlightenment – became 'Dharma'; and one's actions, especially one's communication, became spiritually meaningful – became 'Sangha'.[19]

This brought me from conversion to Buddhism, as represented by Going for Refuge, to conversion *within* Buddhism, as represented by Stream Entry and the Arising of the Will to Enlightenment. It was not enough to orient one's life in the direction of the Three Jewels, or to organize one's life around them, in a general sort of way. It was not even enough to be transformed into them. The transformation had to be made permanent. There had to be a permanent shift of the centre of one's being, a shift from conditioned existence to the Unconditioned; there had to be a permanent switch over from the Round to the Spiral – and this was what was meant by Stream Entry. The greater part of my second lecture on 'The Meaning of Conversion in Buddhism' was therefore devoted to explaining what was meant by the Round and the Spiral, which involved dealing with such topics as the principle of conditionality, the two kinds of conditionality (i.e. the cyclical and the progressive), the Tibetan Wheel of Life, the twelve nidanas, the cause process and the effect process, the three junctures, the twelve positive nidanas, the Path of Vision, the three characteristics of mundane existence, and the three fetters. Similarly, the greater part of my third lecture, on the Arising of the Will to Enlightenment, was devoted to explaining what was meant by Enlightenment (*bodhi*), by Will (*citta*), and by Arising (*utpada*). According to tradition, there were three kinds (or grades) of Bodhi or Enlightenment, and these I reduced to two: Enlightenment which was gained but not communicated, and Enlightenment which was both gained and communicated. The Arising of the Will to Enlightenment referred to the second of these, and represented the transition, within the transcendental order, from an individualistic to an altruistic attitude. It represented conversion from subtle spiritual selfhood to a life of complete selflessness.

Since one could hardly go further than that, in my fourth and last lecture I approached the subject of conversion in Buddhism from an entirely fresh point of view and dealt with it in terms of Turning About in the Deepest Seat of Consciousness. 'Paravritti', or Turning About, consisted in turning from a superficial to a profound mode of awareness. According to the *Lankavatara Sutra*, one of the key texts of the Yogacara school, there were eight consciousnesses (*vijnana*) or, more literally, discriminative awarenesses. These were the five sense-consciousnesses, the mind-consciousness, the afflicted, or defiled, mind-consciousness (afflicted by a dualistic outlook, so that it interpreted experience in terms of subject and object, self and world), and the Alaya or Store-Consciousness. The Alaya or Store-Consciousness had two aspects, the relative and the absolute. The relative Alaya consisted of the impressions left by our past experiences, both those of the present life and those of previous lives. These impressions were thought of as seeds: they were not passive but (potentially) active, and could sprout again whenever conditions permitted. The absolute Alaya was Reality itself, conceived as Pure Awareness, free from all trace of subject-object duality. Turning About took place on the borderline between the relative Alaya and the absolute Alaya. As a result of our performing religious actions, pure seeds, as they were called, were deposited in the relative Alaya, and when enough of these had been accumulated, the

93

absolute Alaya acted upon them in such a way that they pushed out the impure seeds deposited by our mundane actions. This pushing out constituted the Turning About in the Deepest Seat of Consciousness (i.e. in the Alaya) and brought about the transformation of the entire vijnana system, the five sense consciousnesses being collectively transformed into the All-Performing Wisdom, the mind-consciousness into the Distinguishing Wisdom, the afflicted mind-consciousness into the Wisdom of Equality, and the relative Alaya into the Mirror-like Wisdom. The absolute Alaya did not need to be transformed and was equated with the Wisdom of the Dharmadhatu. Thus in terms of Turning About in the Deepest Seat of Consciousness conversion in Buddhism consisted in turning from a dualistic to a non-dualistic mode of awareness and bringing about a radical transformation of one's entire being.

By dealing with conversion to (and within) Buddhism in terms of Going for Refuge, Stream Entry, the Arising of the Will to Enlightenment, and Turning About in the Deepest Seat of Consciousness, I made it clear that all were aspects of a single process. This process was, of course, the process of conversion. Since Going for Refuge was an aspect of conversion, and since Stream Entry was also an aspect of conversion, Going for Refuge and Stream Entry could therefore in principle be equated, as could Going for Refuge and the Arising of the Will to Enlightenment.

94

Though in my lectures on 'The Meaning of Conversion in Buddhism' I did not explicitly make the equation, and was not to do so for a few more years, in the lecture on the Arising of the Will to Enlightenment I came close to doing so. Having reduced the three kinds (or grades) of Enlightenment to two – that is, Enlightenment which was gained but not communicated and Enlightenment which was both gained and communicated – I went on to lay it down as an axiom (and in my notes the words are italicized) that *A spiritual experience which can be kept to oneself is not the same as one which "has" to be communicated, i.e. one whose very nature involves communication.* This meant, in effect, the abolition of the distinction between the two kinds (or grades) of Enlightenment (keeping a spiritual or transcendental experience to oneself was in fact a contradiction in terms), which meant the abolition of the distinction between Going for Refuge and the Arising of the Will to Enlightenment, for the Enlightenment in respect of which the Will to Enlightenment arose was none other than the Enlightenment that was the ultimate object of Going for Refuge. The Arising of the Will to Enlightenment did not carry on from where Going for Refuge left off, so to speak (for Going for Refuge did not 'leave off' at all) but was what I subsequently called the altruistic dimension of Going for Refuge. Similarly with Going for Refuge and Stream Entry. Stream Entry, too, did not carry on from where Going for Refuge left off, but was Going for Refuge itself on a higher, transcendental plane: it was what I subsequently called 'real Going for Refuge', as distinct from the 'provisional Going for Refuge' which was merely cultural and formal and the 'effective Going for Refuge' from which one could still fall away. Thus with the help of the conception of conversion I paved the way, in my four lectures on 'The Meaning of Conversion in Buddhism', for that radical reduction of Stream Entry and the Arising of the Will to Enlightenment – and even of Turning About in the Deepest Seat of Consciousness – to Going for Refuge which characterized my later Buddhist thinking and constituted one of the principal foundations of the WBO and the FWBO (Triratna Buddhist Community).

16

Founding the Western Buddhist Order

In the last section but one I related how, at the end of my first two years in England, I came to the conclusion that a new Buddhist movement was badly needed in Britain. Having paid my farewell visit to India and having returned to England for good in March 1967 (this time *not* at the invitation of the English Sangha Trust) I therefore set about creating that new Buddhist movement, and after a year of preliminary work founded the Western Buddhist Order which, in the opening words of this paper, 'came into existence on Sunday 7 April 1968, when in the course of a ceremony held at Centre House, London, nine men and three women committed themselves to the Path of the Buddha by publicly "taking" the Three Refuges and Ten Precepts from me in the traditional manner.' Thus we have now come full circle, so to speak. We have returned to the point from which we set out – the point, that is to say, at which twelve people's understanding of what was meant by Going for Refuge coincided, at least to some extent, with the understanding at which I myself had arrived after traversing the stages in the history of my Going for Refuge so far described.

But why did my – why did *our* – new Buddhist movement take precisely the form that it did? Why did I found an *order* rather than the more usual society, with its general membership, annual subscriptions, democratically elected office-bearers, and so on? In order to answer this question I shall have to go back a little.

During my long stay in India I had observed that the Buddhist movement there for the most part consisted, organizationally speaking, of a number of Buddhist societies, and that these societies did not always live up to their name. On looking into the matter more closely I discovered that this was due not so much to ordinary human weakness as to the fact that some of the office-bearers and other influential members of the societies in question were not even nominally Buddhists, and had joined their respective organizations for reasons that had little or nothing to do with Buddhism. This was not to say that they were necessarily bad people: some of them were very good people; but the fact that they were not committed Buddhists, and made no serious effort to understand and practise the Dharma, meant that the Buddhist societies of which they were a part could not be run with the energy and inspiration that alone could make them worthy of their name. The basic reason for this unsatisfactory state of affairs was that membership of these societies, as of others similarly constituted, was open to anyone who cared to fill in a form and pay the membership fee. During my long stay in India I had therefore become convinced that it was not really possible for a Buddhist movement to consist, organizationally speaking, of a society or societies (the expression 'Buddhist society' was in fact virtually a contradiction in terms), but that it had to consist, essentially, of a group or groups of committed Buddhists, and my recent experiences in England had left me more convinced of this than ever. It was therefore an order, in the sense of a Sangha or spiritual community, that I founded on Sunday 7 April 1968.

As must have been obvious to those who were present, though they may not have realized the significance of the fact at the time, this Order of ours – the Western Buddhist Order – was what I subsequently termed a unified order. It was a unified order in that it consisted of both men and women, who went for Refuge to the same Three Jewels, observed the same Ten Precepts, practised the same meditations and other spiritual disciplines, and who, where qualified, performed the same administrative and 'ministerial' functions. The Western Buddhist Order was also a unified order in that it was envisaged as consisting of people of different lifestyles and different degrees of commitment to the Three Jewels. Since it was a unified order, and especially since it consisted of both men and women, the Western Buddhist Order represented something of a departure from Eastern Buddhist tradition, at least as that tradition was understood in some parts of the Buddhist world. In all other respects, however, it was fully traditional in structure, as I was carefully to point out towards the end of my lecture on 'The Idea of the Western Buddhist Order and of Upasaka Ordination', the first of the two lectures I gave on that historic day, when after summarizing the history of Buddhism in Britain and explaining the meaning of Going for Refuge I dealt with the four grades of ordination of which the Western Buddhist Order was to consist.

These four grades of ordination, representing four increasing degrees of commitment to the Three Jewels, were those of (1) the upasaka/upasika, the lay brother or lay sister, (2) the maha upasaka/upasika, the senior lay brother or lay sister, (3) the (novice) Bodhisattva, and (4) the bhikshu or monk. Since it was the upasaka/upasika ordination that the twelve ordinands were to receive that evening I naturally had more to say about this grade of ordination than about the three others, which in any case soon fell into desuetude. An upasaka (or upasika) was one who engaged in upasana or religious practice; literally, he was one who 'sat near' (a teacher), that is, who was a disciple. Thus an upasaka was not just a 'lay Buddhist' in the sense of a purely nominal follower of the Buddha's teaching. Though continuing to lead a secular life, he at the same time tried to purify himself with the help of ten vows, three for body, four for speech, and three for mind. These vows were: (1-3) abstention from taking life, from taking the not-given, and from sexual misconduct – by which body was purified; (4-7) abstention from false, harsh, and frivolous speech, as well as from slander and back-biting – by which speech was purified; and (8-10) abstention from covetousness, animosity, and false views – by which mind was purified. Upasaka ordination consisted, essentially, in taking these ten vows preceded by the Three Refuges or, as I had called them earlier in the lecture, the Three Commitments. An upasaka member of the Western Buddhist Order was also expected to be a vegetarian (or at least to make an effort to be one), to practise right livelihood (the fifth constituent of the Buddha's Noble Eightfold Path), and to lead a simple life, as well as to meditate every day, attend a class every week, and go on retreat every year. On a more 'mundane' level, he or she was expected to give whatever practical help he or she could, whether financial or otherwise, to the new Buddhist movement of which the Western Buddhist Order was now the heart and centre. These additional requirements were not embodied in any rule but were left to the discretion of the individual upasaka.

Having dealt with the upasaka/upasika ordination in this way, I emphasized that it represented a very definite degree of commitment indeed. Though

the upasaka grade was in one sense the lowest of the
Order's four grades of ordination, in another sense it
was the most important, for it was the basis on which
the whole structure rested – an insight that may well
have foreshadowed the later absorption of the second,
third, and fourth grades of ordination into the first,
and the renaming of that as the dharmachari ordination. Foreshadowing or not foreshadowing, it was to
the three remaining grades of ordination that I now
turned.

The maha upasaka/upasika, the senior (literally 'great') lay brother or lay sister, was an upasaka
of several years standing. He or she had a certain
amount of understanding and experience of the
Dharma and was able to help out with the giving of
lectures and taking of classes. He or she was, however,
still a householder in the sense of still having a family
and a full-time job. The Bodhisattva in the full traditional sense was one who aimed at the attainment of
Enlightenment for the benefit of all sentient beings.
He was one who took the Bodhisattva vow, and in
the Mahayana the taking of this vow was associated with a definite ordination. In the context of the
Western Buddhist Order, the Bodhisattva was one
who showed signs of possessing exceptional spiritual
gifts, and who was only technically a layman. Though
he or she might have a part-time job, he or she would
function in a 'ministerial' capacity. The bhikshu or
monk was the (celibate) full-timer. He might devote

himself to teaching the Dharma, to study and literary work, or to meditation, or to a combination of two or three of these. In any case, his material needs would be supplied by other members of the order and by the general – that is, the general Buddhist – public. (I spoke of the bhikshu or monk, and not of the bhikshu or monk and the bhikshuni or nun, because it was widely believed in the Buddhist world that the tradition of bhikshuni ordination had died out many centuries ago and could not be renewed. With the absorption of the three higher grades of ordination in the first and the emergence within the Western Buddhist Order of anagarikas or (celibate) 'homeless ones' of both sexes this ceased to be a problem for our new Buddhist movement, if indeed it had ever been one.)

Though the greater part of my lecture was devoted to explaining the meaning of Going for Refuge and dealing with the four grades of ordination, I also touched on a number of other topics. Apart from issues of a more general nature such as the connection between Western Buddhism and the events of the age in which my audience and I were living, these included the difference between the academic study of Buddhism and actual commitment to the Three Jewels, the importance of spiritual fellowship and spiritual community, and the inability of Buddhist societies to meet the growing needs of Western Buddhists, as well as the reasons that had led to the establishment of the

Western Buddhist Order. It had been established, I declared, to enable people to commit themselves more fully to the Buddhist way of life, to provide opportunities for spiritual fellowship, and to provide an 'organizational' base for the propagation of Buddhism in the United Kingdom. I also took note, before describing the structure of the Western Buddhist Order, of a difference of opinion on the subject of Sangha or spiritual community. There were, I said, two extreme views. According to one view, the Sangha consisted only of monks; the rest were not really Buddhists at all, their duty being merely to support the monks. Buddhism was in fact a purely monastic religion, and a 'Buddhist laity' a contradiction in terms. According to the other view, the Sangha consisted of the entire population of a Buddhist country. Thieves, prostitutes, drunkards, and policemen – all were Buddhists. They were 'born Buddhists', and in my experience 'born Buddhists' knew nothing of Buddhism. These, then, were the two extreme views: one too narrow, and the other too broad. So far as the Western Buddhist Order was concerned, it was proposed to follow a middle way between them, as would be evident from its very structure. Having described this structure, and having said a few words about the 'Friends' of the Western Buddhist Order, I concluded the lecture by saying that I had explained the idea of the Western Buddhist Order and of upasaka ordination in some detail because of its extreme importance, and because it was probably the biggest step yet taken by British Buddhism.

In the second of my two lectures of the day, on 'The Bodhisattva Vow', I dealt with the Bodhisattva ideal, and particularly the Bodhisattva vow itself, as exemplifying the way in which we rose above the pairs of opposites, and in this connection gave a straightforward exposition of the Arising of the Will to Enlightenment, the Sevenfold Puja, the Four Great Vows, and the Six Paramitas. Thus my second lecture was less closely connected with the actual ordination ceremony than was my first. Towards the end of it I did, however, say a few words about the Bodhisattva ordination, which was of course the third grade of ordination in the Western Buddhist Order. I also referred to the fact that I had myself taken the Bodhisattva ordination from Dhardo Rimpoche, whom I described as perhaps embodying the Bodhisattva ideal to a greater extent than any other person I had known. It was my hope, I concluded, that in the course of time a few people in Britain would be ready to take the Bodhisattva ordination, in which case our Western Buddhist Order would be well underway. But whether they took the Bodhisattva ordination or not, everybody present should try to imbibe the Bodhisattva spirit and echo the Bodhisattva vow in their own hearts.

So far as I remember, the main reason for my speaking on the Bodhisattva vow that day, apart from the fact that the Bodhisattva ordination formed part of the structure of the Western Buddhist Order, was that I wanted to emphasize the altruistic and other-regarding aspect of Buddhism and the Buddhist spiritual life. Though I had not yet explicitly identified the Arising of the Will to Enlightenment as the altruistic dimension of Going for Refuge, I was well aware that in the individualistic and self-regarding atmosphere of British Buddhism the act of Going for Refuge, and therewith the upasaka/upasika ordination, was likely to be understood as possessing significance only for the person immediately concerned, and that it was therefore necessary to introduce a 'Mahayana' element into the proceedings. It was almost as if, having not as yet established a direct connection between the Arising of the Will to Enlightenment and Going for Refuge, I at least wanted the Bodhisattva ideal to 'be around' and ready to enter into the situation as soon as conditions permitted.

The founding of the Western Buddhist Order was not only an important stage in the process whereby the significance and value of Going for Refuge became clear to me. It also marked the beginning of a new phase in that process. Though I had realized that Going for Refuge was the central act of the Buddhist life, and that it meant organizing one's existence round the Three Jewels, that realization had so far found expression only in my personal life and in my writings and lectures, and even then only to a very limited extent. But now the situation was entirely changed. The twelve people who made up the Western Buddhist Order had 'taken' the Three Refuges and Ten Precepts from me – had been ordained as upasakas and upasikas by me – and their understanding of the meaning of Going for Refuge coincided with mine, at least partly. Like one lamp lighting a dozen others, I had been able to share with them my realization of the absolute centrality of the act of Going for Refuge, and henceforth that realization would find expression not in my life only but also in theirs. Not that the realization in question was something fixed and final. It could continue to grow and develop, and find expression in a hundred ways as yet unthought-of. Unfortunately, some founder members of the Western Buddhist Order found it difficult to appreciate this fact, or even to sustain their original commitment, and before long either resigned from the Order or withdrew from active participation in its affairs. Their places were, however, soon filled and more than filled, and I had the satisfaction of lighting first scores, and then hundreds of lamps, and the still greater satisfaction of seeing them, together with those lamps that had burned undimmed from the beginning, grow brighter as my own lamp grew brighter. In other words, I had the satisfaction of knowing that in founding the Western Buddhist Order I had founded a Sangha or spiritual community that not only shared my realization that

Going for Refuge was the central and definitive act of the Buddhist life, but also shared, in the person of at least some of its members, my conviction that that realization itself was capable of continued growth and development.

With the founding of the Western Buddhist Order my own Going for Refuge thus became bound up with the Going for Refuge of a number of other people, so that from this time onwards my History will be covering ground with which many Order members are already familiar. In the sections that follow I shall, therefore, be more selective and more succinct.

17
The Wider Context

The act of Going for Refuge is an individual act, that is, it is an act of the individual. But it is not only an act of the individual. It is also an act that can be performed by a number of people, and these people may have the same (individual) understanding of its meaning, the same (individual) realization of its significance, in which case they together form a Sangha or spiritual community, as in the case of the Western Buddhist Order. Where there is a Sangha or spiritual community, therefore, the individual's act of Going for Refuge is one of a number of such acts, all of which take place within a common framework – a framework of which the individual who Goes for Refuge is himself a part. Thus although the act of Going for Refuge is an individual act it is, at the same time, an act that takes place within a wider context, that is, a context wider than the individual's own personal life. Indeed it is from that wider context that the act of Going for Refuge derives part of its significance or, as one might also say, it is because it takes place in this wider context that the act of Going for Refuge is able to reveal itself more fully. About the time that I founded the WBO and FWBO I started giving serious thought to the question of the nature of this wider context. Though my thinking was not very systematic, I soon realized that Going for Refuge in fact took place within a three-fold context, or rather, within three quite different contexts, all of which were interconnected. These three contexts may be termed, very provisionally, the social or communal, the higher-evolutionary, and the cosmic.

The social or communal context of Going for Refuge is, of course, the Sangha or spiritual community as I have already indicated. Between a spiritual community and what I term a group there is a world of difference. Whereas a group consists of 'group members', or those who are self-conscious (i.e. self-aware) only in a very rudimentary way, and whose attitudes and behaviour are determined entirely by those of the group, a spiritual community consists of (true) individuals, or those who are self-conscious, independent, sensitive, emotionally positive, responsible, and creative. Unfortunately, the English language has no proper term for individuals of this sort and consequently no proper term for the kind of 'group' to which they 'belong', so that it is extremely difficult to explain the nature of the difference between a group and a spiritual community and extremely difficult, therefore, to explain the nature of the spiritual community itself. It is also extremely difficult to explain the nature of the consciousness or awareness that characterizes the spiritual community as such. This consciousness is not the sum total of the individual consciousnesses concerned, nor even a kind of collective consciousness, but a consciousness of an entirely different order for which we have no word in English, but to which the Russian word *sobornost* perhaps gives a clue. At the stage of this History with which I am now concerned I started thinking of this 'third' order of consciousness in terms of the transcendental Bodhicitta or Will to Enlightenment. I saw the Bodhicitta as arising within the Sangha or spiritual community as a whole rather than as being an individual's personal possession, so to speak. Similarly, I saw the Sangha or spiritual community as being the reflection of the ideal figure of the Bodhisattva or 'personified' Bodhicitta. By the time of my 1973 'sabbatical' I had come to see our new Buddhist movement, particularly the Western Buddhist Order, as constituting a tiny reflection of the Bodhisattva Avalokitesvara, the Bodhisattva of Compassion, in his eleven-headed and thousand-armed form. Each member of the Order was, in fact, one of Avalokitesvara's arms (or hands), for each Order member went for Refuge, and the Bodhicitta – whose various beneficent activities those arms symbolized – was the altruistic dimension of Going for Refuge. Thus in the same way that each of Avalokitesvara's arms formed part of his body, so the act of Going

111

for Refuge took place within the wider context of the Sangha or spiritual community, which was the Bodhisattva's reflection – even, in a sense, his embodiment – or within the wider context of the 'third' order of consciousness. Strictly speaking, I should have thought of this 'third' order of consciousness not so much in terms of the transcendental Bodhicitta as in terms of transcendental Going for Refuge, just as I should have thought of the Sangha or spiritual community as being the reflection not so much of the 'personified' Bodhicitta as of the 'personified' Going for Refuge; but since Buddhist tradition had not 'personified' Going for Refuge in an ideal figure, and surrounded that figure with myth and symbol, in the way that it had done with the Bodhicitta, it was not really possible for me to do so – nor, in the last analysis, was it really necessary. Inasmuch as the Bodhicitta was the altruistic dimension of Going for Refuge, whatever was said of the Bodhicitta could also be said – *mutatis mutandis* – of Going for Refuge.

The higher-evolutionary context of Going for Refuge, as I have termed it, is Buddhism conceived of as corresponding to – even as coinciding with – the upper reaches of the total evolutionary process. Towards the end of 1969 I gave a series of eight lectures entitled 'The Higher Evolution of Man'. In these lectures, which were in part based on lectures given three years earlier, I divided the evolutionary process into two main sections, one of which I termed the

Lower Evolution and the other the Higher Evolution. Man, in the sense of the self-conscious or self-aware human being, occupied a point midway between the two. The Lower Evolution represented what he had developed out of, the Higher Evolution what he could develop into. The Lower Evolution was the process of development from amoeba to man, and was covered by the sciences, especially biology; The Higher Evolution was the process of development from man to Buddha, and was covered by psychology, by the fine arts, and by religion. The Lower Evolution was collective, the Higher Evolution individual. Buddhism, as a universal religion, that is a religion that addressed itself to the individual and affirmed individual rather than collective values, belonged to the Higher Evolution. In the fifth lecture in this series I indeed spoke of Buddhism as the Path of the Higher Evolution, that is, I spoke of it as representing a continuation, on increasingly higher levels, of the evolutionary process itself. It was the evolutionary process become, in the person of the individual, self-conscious or self-aware. This was not the way in which we usually thought of Buddhism, but it was what Buddhism essentially was. In Buddhism there were many doctrines and disciplines, many moral rules and devotional observances, but they were all secondary. Even meditation was secondary. What was important, for Buddhism, was that man should grow and develop – that he should evolve. Buddhism was not a matter of thinking and knowing, or even of doing, but of being and becoming. In other words Buddhism was a matter of following the Path of the Higher Evolution.

As I was careful to point out, such a way of looking at Buddhism was fully in accordance with the Buddha's own teaching, and in this connection I referred to the Mahaprajapati incident (the Dharma was 'whatever conduced to one's spiritual growth and development'), as well as to the simile of the lotus flowers in various stages of unfoldment and to the parable of the herbs and plants, otherwise known as the parable of the rain-cloud. With so much emphasis on growth and development it was not surprising that the image of the Path should have been at the very centre of the Buddha's teaching, or that Buddhism itself should have been a Path – the Path to Enlightenment or nirvana. There were many different formulations of this Path, but the one that brought out most clearly the fact that Buddhism was essentially a Path, and that this Path was the Path of the Higher Evolution, was that of the twelve positive nidanas, and it was with this particular formulation of the Path that I wanted to deal on that occasion. The last third of the lecture therefore consisted of a detailed exposition of the twelve positive nidanas or links, from suffering/faith to freedom/knowledge of the destruction of the asravas.

The reason why this particular formulation is able to bring out so clearly the fact that Buddhism is essentially a Path, and that this Path is the Path of the Higher Evolution, is that it consists of a progressive series of mental and spiritual states or experiences – a series wherein each state or experience arises in dependence on the one immediately preceding. Since the Higher Evolution consists in the development of progressively higher states of consciousness, just as the Lower Evolution consists in the development of progressively more complex material forms, it is obvious that there is a correspondence between the twelve positive nidanas and the process of the Higher Evolution. Indeed, it is obvious that in principle the twelve positive nidanas and the process of the Higher Evolution actually coincide, so that in causing the mental and spiritual states or experiences represented by the nidanas to arise within oneself – or rather, in causing oneself to *become* them – one is at the same time participating in the higher-evolutionary process. Now the first two positive nidanas are suffering (*dukkha*, Skt. *duhkha*) and faith (*saddha*, Skt. *sraddha*), for in dependence on suffering there arises 'faith', and this faith – as I made clear in the lecture itself – is faith in the Three Jewels, as representing the highest values of existence. It is our *total* response to those values, and as such it manifests as actual commitment to them, that is, manifests as Going for Refuge. Thus the act of Going for Refuge is identical with the arising of faith in dependence on suffering, the more especially since one Goes for Refuge *from* those

115

very things on account of the painful and unsatisfactory nature of which one goes in quest of higher
values. This means that the act of Going for Refuge
takes place within the series of mental and spiritual
states or experiences represented by the twelve positive nidanas and, therefore, within the wider context
of the higher-evolutionary process. Not that the act
of Going for Refuge is limited to the second positive
nidana. The series of the twelve positive nidanas is not
only a progressive but also a cumulative series, so that
the subsequent positive nidanas arise in proximate or
remote dependence on faith in the Three Jewels and,
therefore, on the act of Going for Refuge.

Just as the social or communal context of Going
for Refuge is connected with the Bodhicitta, and
the higher-evolutionary context with the Path, so
what I have termed the cosmic context of Going
for Refuge is connected with the Bodhisattva ideal
in the broadest sense. Originally, there was only one
Bodhisattva, who was the Buddha himself during
the pre-Enlightenment phase of his career, that
phase being first understood as comprising the first
thirty-five years of his life and then understood as
comprising the whole series of his previous existences
as recorded in the Jataka or 'Birth' Stories. Later, after
the Bodhisattva ideal had come to be regarded as the
ultimate spiritual ideal for all Buddhists, even for all
human beings, the Bodhisattvas multiplied and their
unwearied activities were seen as extending through

infinite time and infinite space, as we saw in section 13, when I spoke of *The Two Buddhist Books in Mahayana* and of 'The Vows of the Bodhisattva Samantabhadra'. Eventually, the figure of the Bodhisattva was seen as transcending history altogether and he, she, they, or it became the 'personification(s)' of a cosmic principle. Some years later I termed this principle the Bodhisattva principle, or principle of perpetual self-transcendence, but at this stage of my History I more often spoke of it as the Cosmic Bodhicitta or Cosmic Will to Enlightenment, as I did in my 1969 lecture 'The Awakening of the Bodhi Heart'. It is the reflection of this same Cosmic Bodhicitta that, appearing in the psyche-continuum of the individual, is the Bodhicitta in the more usual sense of the term. Since this latter Bodhicitta is the altruistic dimension of Going for Refuge, as I have more than once observed, the reflection of the Cosmic Bodhicitta also appears as the act of Going for Refuge (the two reflections are in fact one), so that the individual's act of Going for Refuge takes place within the Cosmic Bodhicitta and, therefore, within the wider context of the Bodhisattva ideal in the broadest sense.

In speaking of the act of Going for Refuge as taking place within a wider context, whether that of the Sangha or spiritual community, the Path, or the Bodhisattva ideal in the broadest sense, I do not mean to suggest that it takes place within it as a high dive might take place within the four walls of an indoor swimming pool. Between the act of Going for Refuge and the context within which it takes place there is an organic connection – a connection which I tried to express, at the beginning of this section, by speaking of the individual who Goes for Refuge as being himself a part of the common framework within which he and others Go for Refuge. Because there is this organic connection the act of Going for Refuge is able to reveal itself – that is, reveal its nature and significance – more fully. Because there is this organic connection the act of Going for Refuge is also able, as the reflection, in the individual, of the wider context within which that act takes place, to reveal something of the nature and significance of the wider context itself.

18
Levels of Going for Refuge

In *A Survey of Buddhism* I drew attention to the fact that Going for Refuge is not an act to be done once and for all time, but that it is something which grows with one's understanding of Buddhism. Thus not only does the act of Going for Refuge take place within a wider context; it also takes place on different levels, passage from one to another of which constitutes one's spiritual life as a Buddhist. According to tradition there are two levels of Going for Refuge, the mundane and the transcendental, but in a talk on 'Going for Refuge' which I gave in 1978, at the Western Buddhist Order's tenth anniversary convention, I distinguished altogether six. This talk was given on 3 April, which means that it was given almost exactly ten years ago, and my six levels of Going for Refuge were the cultural, the provisional, the effective, the real, the ultimate, and the cosmic.

Before describing these levels I reminisced for a few minutes about my own experience of 'formal' Going for Refuge, that is, my own experience of reciting the words of the Three Refuges and the Five (or Ten) Precepts, prior to the founding of the Western

Buddhist Order, and in this connection described six different incidents, some of which I have dealt with in the first half of this paper. These incidents, like many others I could have mentioned, showed that appreciation of the real significance of Going for Refuge was rather lacking in Buddhist circles in the East, and even in Buddhist circles in the West. The Refuges were simply something one recited, or something that showed one was a Buddhist, in the merely social sense. They were a sort of flag that was waved on special occasions. If one went to the temple on Wesak day, one recited the Refuges, as one also did when there was a wedding, or a name-giving ceremony, or a memorial service, or a public meeting. Not that there was anything wrong with reciting the Refuges, I hastened to add. The trouble was that people generally recited them without thinking about their meaning. In my experience it was only the Tibetans who had any appreciation of what Going for Refuge really meant, or any realization of its tremendous – indeed its central – importance in and for the Buddhist life. Elsewhere in the Buddhist world people seemed to have forgotten its importance. True, they recited the Refuges often enough (and it was good that they recited them), but hardly ever did they actually *Go for Refuge*. This was really surprising. The significance of Going for Refuge was clear enough from the Buddhist scriptures, especially from the Pali scriptures. Time and again in those scriptures did one find the Buddha giving a teaching, and time and again did one find the recipient of that teaching responding to his words with exclamations of amazement and wonder and with the heartfelt declaration 'I Go for Refuge to the Buddha, to his Dharma, and to his Sangha!' This was no mere recitation of a formula. It was the response of one's total being to the Truth. One committed oneself to the Truth, surrendered to the Truth, wanted to devote one's whole life to the Truth, and this effect could be produced not only by the hearing of the Dharma but also by the sight of the Buddha or the sight of the Sangha – or even by the sight of a team of Order members and Mitras at work.

Thus the importance of Going for Refuge was clear from the Buddhist scriptures, even though the greater part of the Buddhist world might have forgotten it, and having shown this I turned to my six levels of Going for Refuge. Cultural Going for Refuge, which could also be called formal or ethnic Going for Refuge, was the Going for Refuge of those Eastern Buddhists who did not actually follow Buddhism as a spiritual teaching (though they might be positively influenced by it on the social level), and who made no effort to evolve spiritually, but who were nonetheless very proud of Buddhism as part of their cultural heritage and who definitely considered themselves (ethnic) Buddhists. Such people recited the Refuges as an affirmation of their cultural and national identity and even went so far as to claim that they were 'born Buddhists', though in truth one could no more be a born Buddhist than one could (according to the Buddha) be a born brahmin. In our own Movement there was no cultural Going for Refuge because no one was a 'born Buddhist', but there was, perhaps, something like it when someone was attracted to the Movement as a 'positive group' and happily joined in everything we did, including chanting the Refuges. Provisional Going for Refuge went beyond cultural Going for Refuge, but fell short of effective Going for Refuge. Here someone who was a 'born Buddhist', in the sense of having been born into Buddhist surroundings, started taking Buddhism seriously to some extent, even started practising it to some extent, but did not really commit himself (or herself) either to Buddhism or to his (or her) own spiritual development. He or she might, however, be aware of the possibility, even the desirability, of committing oneself, and might be thinking of doing so later on. In our own Movement this level of Going for Refuge was represented by the Mitra, who regarded himself (or herself) as 'belonging' to the FWBO, who meditated regularly, who helped out in various practical ways, and who might be thinking of ordination.

Effective Going for Refuge consisted of actually committing oneself to the Three Jewels. Since I was addressing a gathering of Order members there was no need for me to elaborate, as I indeed remarked at the time, for they all knew very well what effective

Going for Refuge meant and that it corresponded to upasaka/upasika ordination in the Western Buddhist Order. I therefore confined myself to saying a few words about the esoteric Refuges, that is, the Guru, the Deva, and the Dakini – particularly about the Dakini. Before so doing, however, I pointed out that while effective Going for Refuge corresponded to upasaka/upasika ordination in the Western Buddhist Order the traditional Buddhist socio-religious categories were, in fact, becoming less and less relevant to us. Perhaps it would be better if we spoke not in terms of upasaka/upasika ordination but simply of 'ordination' or even of 'threefold commitment' (i.e. commitment with body, speech, and mind) – a speculation that no doubt foreshadowed the development with which I shall be dealing in section 20. Real Going for Refuge took place when one developed insight and wisdom and thus entered upon the transcendental Path or, in other words, became a Stream Entrant. In traditional terms real Going for Refuge was transcendental Going for Refuge, all the previous refuges – even effective Going for Refuge – being mundane, which was quite a sobering thought. Until one had entered the Stream one could fall back: could leave the spiritual community – resign from the Order. For this reason a positive, spiritually supportive environment was of the utmost importance – at least until such time as one entered the Stream. Ultimate Going for Refuge occurred when one attained Enlightenment.

On this level one did not go to any outside Refuge, but was one's own Refuge. In fact, on this level there was neither inside nor outside, neither self nor other.

Cosmic Going for Refuge was not exactly another level of Going for Refuge but referred to the evolutionary process, that is, referred to the Lower Evolution and the Higher Evolution. First came the amoeba, then the mollusc, then the fish, the reptile, the bird, and the mammal. Finally there came man – *Homo sapiens*. Looking at this process, what one in fact saw was a Going for Refuge. Each form of life aspired to develop into a higher form or, so to speak, went for Refuge to that higher form. This might sound impossibly poetic, but it was what one in fact saw. In man the evolutionary process became conscious of itself; this was the Higher Evolution. When the Higher Evolution became conscious of itself (and it became conscious of itself in and through the spiritually committed individual) this was Going for Refuge in the sense of effective Going for Refuge. Through our Going for Refuge we are united, as it were, with all living beings, who in their own way, and on their own level, in a sense also went for Refuge. Thus Going for Refuge was not simply a particular devotional practice or even a threefold act of individual commitment, but the key to the mystery of existence.

Three or four years later I gave another talk on 'Going for Refuge'. The talk was given in Bombay, to a mixed audience of Theosophists and 'ex-Untouchable'

Buddhists, and in it I approached the subject via my experience of our new Buddhist movement in the West, involvement with which culminated in 'joining the Order' or, in more traditional terms, Going for Refuge to the Buddha, the Dharma, and the Sangha. In the course of this talk I distinguished only four levels of Going for Refuge: the provisional, the effective, the real, and the absolute (= the ultimate), ethnic Going for Refuge being subsumed under provisional Going for Refuge, and cosmic Going for Refuge being omitted. Real Going for Refuge was, however, correlated with the opening of the Dharma-eye, or Eye of Truth, the third of the Five Eyes of Buddhist tradition, and this in turn with (transcendental) Going for Refuge and with Stream Entry. Indeed, having discussed the three fetters (i.e. self-view, doubt, and dependence on moral rules and religious observances), the breaking of which was equivalent to Stream Entry, and distinguished between commitment and lifestyle, I raised the question of the nature of the relation between the arising of the Bodhicitta, Going for Refuge, the opening of the Dharma-eye, Stream Entry, and Going Forth, and explained it as follows:

The Bodhicitta, or the arising of the Bodhicitta, represents, we may say, the more 'altruistic' dimension of these four other experiences. Or rather, all five of them, including the Bodhicitta itself, represent the five different aspects of a single basic, crucial and unique spiritual experience. The Going for Refuge draws attention to the emotional and volitional aspect of this experience, the opening of the Dharma-eye to the Unconditioned depth of its cognitive content, Stream Entry to the permanent and far-reaching nature of its effects, while Going Forth into homelessness draws attention to the extent of the reorganization which, regardless of whether or not one becomes a monk in the formal sense, the experience inevitably brings about in the pattern of one's daily life. As for the Bodhicitta it represents, as I have said, the altruistic or 'other-regarding' aspect of the experience.[20]

19
Going for Refuge Old and New

In December 1973 I held the first of what was to be a long series of FWBO study retreats, as they came to be called. On these retreats I would take a group of Order members and others through a Buddhist text, discussing it line by line and word by word and trying to relate it to our own understanding and practice of the Dharma. Most of the texts we studied were classics of Buddhist literature, canonical and non-canonical, but a few were modern works. Among the latter was Nyanaponika Thera's essay *The Threefold Refuge*, on which I held a study retreat at 'Padmaloka' in the autumn of 1978. Nyanaponika Thera was a Theravadin monk of German extraction who had resided in Kandy since 1952, and who had been largely responsible for founding and running the Buddhist Publication Society. His essay dated from 1948. In it he not only explored the meaning of Going for Refuge from the standpoint of a liberal Theravadin but also tried, as it seemed, to find a way of reviving the practice of Going for Refuge as an act of individual commitment to the Three Jewels, and it was mainly for this reason that I decided to hold a study retreat on this work.

The Threefold Refuge was divided into two parts. Part I consisted of an abridged translation of Buddhaghosa's exposition of a passage in the *Majjhima-Nikaya* dealing with the Refuges, Part II of Nyanaponika's own thoughts and comments. The latter fell into two sections. In the first section Nyanaponika made some general comments on the subject of Going for Refuge, while in the second he commented on Buddhaghosa's exposition of the sutta passage. Instead of going through the work in regular order, which would have meant plunging straight into Buddhaghosa's rather scholastic exposition, we studied first Nyanaponika's general comments on Going for Refuge, then Buddhaghosa's exposition, and finally Nyanaponika's comments on that exposition, which in any case seemed a more logical way of proceeding. In the course of our study a number of topics arose and were discussed. While these did not always relate directly to the subject of Going for Refuge, they invariably had a definite bearing on one or another aspect of the spiritual life. Among the topics discussed were the difference between passivity and receptivity, the beauty of 'the spiritual', emotional self-indulgence, love and power, authority, (irrational) guilt, immanence, 'making merit', magic and technology, and the difficulty of reforming a religion that has become corrupt.

For the most part, however, our discussion revolved around Nyanaponika's exploration of the meaning of Going for Refuge, both in his own terms and as expounded by Buddhaghosa. With some of his thoughts and comments we found ourselves very much in agreement, as we certainly were when he pointed out that Going for Refuge was, or should be, 'a conscious act, and not the mere profession of a theoretical belief, still less the habitual rite of traditional piety.' Indeed, there were times when the scholarly German monk seemed to be giving expression to our innermost convictions and, what was more, giving expression to them not only with precision but with eloquence. Nonetheless, the more we went through *The Threefold Refuge* the more we became aware that, despite the author's evident sincerity, there was something seriously wrong with his whole approach to Going for Refuge. Though he defined Going for Refuge briefly as *a conscious act of determination, understanding and devotion*, adding that those aspects of taking Refuge '[had] their counterparts in the volitional, rational and emotional sides of the human mind' and that 'for a harmonious development of character the cultivation of all three [was] required',[21] the fact was that in the last analysis Nyanaponika's approach to Going for Refuge tended to be one-sidedly intellectual. He was more aware that devotion needed the support of understanding than aware that understanding needed the support of devotion, and more concerned to emphasize the difference between devotion and blind faith than the

difference between understanding and merely theoretical appreciation. Faith might be explained in terms
of reason, but understanding could not, it seemed, be
explained in terms of emotion. As I observed in the
course of our discussion, Nyanaponika's one-sidedness (and his apparent fear of emotion) may have
been due to the fact that, living and working as he
did in Buddhist Ceylon, surrounded by devout lay
Buddhists who were accustomed to recite the Refuges
and Precepts without thinking about their meaning,
he felt it important to emphasize the aspect of understanding. Alternatively, he may have thought of his
paper as being addressed to Westerners, or at least to
the Western-educated, and therefore assumed that
for such people an intellectual approach to Going
for Refuge was the most appropriate. Whatever
the reason for his one-sidedness may have been,
Nyanaponika's tendency to play down the importance
of emotion was characteristic of his whole attitude
towards Buddhism and the spiritual life, at least so far
as that attitude could be inferred from his paper. He
made no mention of spiritual friendship, and in fact
appeared to see the spiritual life exclusively in terms of
a progressive disillusionment with the imperfections
of conditioned existence instead of seeing it, equally,
in terms of an increasing attraction to and fascination
with the beauty of the Unconditioned.

Perhaps the most interesting part of Nyanaponika's
paper was that in which he dealt with the four kinds

of mundane Going for Refuge described in the expository passage translated in Part I. These four modes of refuge, as he also called them, were the Surrender of Self, the Acceptance of the Guiding Ideal, the Acceptance of Discipleship, and Homage by Prostration, and Buddhaghosa explained the last three of these by reference to scriptural passages in which a particular disciple, having heard the Dharma from the Buddha, went for Refuge using a formula other than the customary 'Buddham saranam gacchami' etc. In Nyanaponika's view the scriptural passages in which reference was made were not very enlightening, and indeed the connection between these passages and the modes of refuge that they supposedly illustrated was not always clear. The first kind of mundane Going for Refuge, the Surrender of Self, Buddhaghosa did not explain by reference to any scriptural passage, though he gave the Refuge-going formula, with which it was traditionally associated. Thus there were not only four kinds of mundane Going for Refuge but also four alternative Refuge-going formulas, which served to emphasize the fact that it is Going for Refuge that matters rather than the particular form of words in which that act finds expression. According to Nyanaponika the four modes of refuge were given in *descending* order (though he was not completely sure of this), 'beginning from the highest form, the complete Self-surrender, and ending with the lowest, the Homage by Prostration',[22] so that it was possible for him to correlate the three lowest modes with the three aspects of Going for Refuge, that is, the emotional, the rational, and the volitional. Homage by Prostration represented the emotional side of taking Refuge, Acceptance of Discipleship the rational, and Acceptance of the Three Jewels as one's Guiding Ideal the volitional. Once again emotion was devalued in relation to reason. As for Surrender of Self, it represented the highest form of Going for Refuge, and Nyanaponika cited from Buddhaghosa's *Visuddhi-magga* or 'Path of Purity' a passage that seemed to indicate that in what he called 'the early days of the Dhamma' it was customary to Go for Refuge in this way, employing the appropriate formula, before asking the guru for a subject of meditation.

This appears to have led Nyanaponika to wonder whether it might not be possible for the formula of Self-surrender to be used by those who, like the meditators of old, wanted to take Buddhism more seriously than did the majority of their co-religionists. Indeed, his conception of Surrender of Self seemed to correspond to Going for Refuge as understood in the Western Buddhist Order – that is, to our upasaka/upasika ordination. In other words, it corresponded to what I called effective Going for Refuge as distinct from cultural or ethnic Going for Refuge; for, as he was at pains to point out, though taking Refuge by way of Self-surrender was still far from the complete abolishing of egotism and self-delusion it

was a powerful means to that end and '[might] mark
the transition from the worldly or mundane refuge
to which it still belong[ed], to the Supermundane
refuge to which it aim[ed].'[23] However, the correspondence between Nyanaponika's conception of
Surrender of Self and Going for Refuge, in the sense
of upasaka/upasika ordination, as understood in the
Western Buddhist Order, was by no means perfect. In
the case of the Western Buddhist Order one not only
went for Refuge as an individual but also found that
one was, by virtue of one's Going for Refuge, one of
a number of people who had also gone for Refuge:
one found that one was a 'member' of a Sangha or
spiritual community, with all that that implied in
the way of spiritual friendship and cooperation. In
Nyanaponika's conception of Buddhism and the spiritual life there was, seemingly, no place for spiritual
community, so that for him Going for Refuge by way
of Self-surrender was an essentially individual affair
and 'the greatest of all vows', as he called the formula of
Self-surrender, was to be taken 'in the secrecy of one's
heart', the presence of any witness to the taking of
the vow being dismissed as 'publicity'. Thus although
Nyanaponika saw that Going for Refuge had become
'the mere profession of a theoretical belief' and 'the
habitual rite of traditional piety', and though he saw
in Surrender of Self the possibility of making Going
for Refuge 'a conscious act', the fact that he was a
Theravadin and living in Ceylon meant that he was

not really able to do very much towards replacing the 'old' (cultural and ethnic) Going for Refuge by a 'new' (more conscious and individual) Going for Refuge.

20
Upasaka into Dharmachari

As I had explained on the day the Western Buddhist Order was founded, upasaka/upasika ordination consisted in taking the Three Refuges and Ten Precepts, and the upasaka/upasika was expected to be a vegetarian, to practise right livelihood, and to lead a simple life. In addition, he or she was expected to meditate daily, to attend classes and go on retreat, and to give practical help to our new Buddhist movement. This was far, far more than was expected of an upasaka or 'lay Buddhist' in most parts of the Buddhist world, as I well knew, but as the years went by, and as Order members increasingly organized their lives round the Three Jewels, the difference between them and the upasakas of the East grew more and more pronounced. So long as the Order was confined to Britain this did not really matter, though the occasional visiting bhikkhu might express his astonishment that 'mere upasakas' should be so devoted to the Dharma and wonder why they were not all in yellow robes. When our new Buddhist movement spread to India, however, and when upasaka/upasika ordinations started being given on Indian soil, the difference between an ordinary 'lay Buddhist' and a member of the Western Buddhist Order – or Trailokya Bauddha Mahasangha, as it was known in India – became more striking than ever. Indeed, the fact that ordinary 'lay Buddhists' and members of the Trailokya Bauddha Mahasangha were called upasakas tended to confuse people and, therefore, to make our work more difficult, so that it soon became obvious that we would have to consider a change of nomenclature.

The Western Buddhist Order was established in India in February and June 1979, in the course of my first two visits to the subcontinent since the founding of our new Buddhist movement in Britain. By the time of my third visit, which took place during the winter of 1981-82 and lasted four months, the Order there had grown in strength and maturity and already the 'ex-Untouchable' Buddhists of central and western India were beginning to look to it for guidance. Indeed the Indian members of the Trailokya Bauddha Mahasangha were themselves 'ex-Untouchables', several of them being old friends and disciples of mine with whom Lokamitra had made contact on his arrival on the scene in 1977. Since my final departure from India in 1967 the followers of Dr Ambedkar had had few opportunities of hearing the Dharma, and though much of the fervour with which they had originally embraced Buddhism remained, the vast majority of them were, unfortunately, Buddhists only in a very nominal sense. Thus their Going for Refuge was, at best, a cultural or ethnic Going for Refuge, so that the difference between them and the upasakas and upasikas of the Western Buddhist Order/Trailokya Bauddha Mahasangha who were by this time working among them was truly enormous. At an Order meeting held in New Bombay in March 1982, and attended by twenty-one Order members (including six of non-Indian origin) I therefore proposed that the terms upasaka and upasika should be dropped and that in future members of the Order should be known as Dharmacharis and Dharmacharinis. Such a change of nomenclature would have several advantages. Besides distinguishing Order members from ordinary 'lay Buddhists', it would serve to underline the difference between cultural or ethnic Going for Refuge and effective Going for Refuge. It would also make it easier for Order members to deal with bhikshus, some of whom were inclined to adopt an arrogant and overbearing attitude towards 'mere upasakas', even when they themselves were making no effort to practise the Dharma.

After a short discussion the meeting accepted my proposal, and in the course of the next few months Order members elsewhere in the world followed suit. Thus took place the transformation of upasaka into Dharmachari and upasika into Dharmacharini.

Whether in its masculine or feminine form, the term by which members of the Western Buddhist Order were henceforth known was not in general use among Buddhists, and it was partly for this reason that we had selected it. At the same time it was a thoroughly traditional term, being found in several places in the scriptures, notably in two successive verses of the *Dhammapada*, in each of which the Buddha declares 'The dhammachari lives happily, (both) in this world and in the world beyond.'[24] Literally, Dharmachari (Skt.) or Dhammachari (Pali) meant 'Dharma-farer' or 'practitioner of the Dharma' (from Dharma + *car*, 'one who walks or lives') and was therefore an exact description of what a member of the Order was or tried to be. It was also analogous in form to such terms as Brahmachari, Bhadrachari, and Khechari, just as Dharmacharya or 'Dharma-faring' was analogous to Bodhicharya. Moreover, by a fortunate coincidence the second of the two *Dhammapada* verses in which the term Dharmachari occurred was one of the three verses from the *Dhammapada* included in the 'Last Vandana', as it was called, a set of Pali verses which the 'ex-Untouchable' Buddhists were in the habit of singing to a solemn and deeply moving melody at the conclusion of meetings, and which we ourselves had already adopted, both in India and elsewhere.

But though upasakas were now known as Dharmacharis and upasikas as Dharmacharinis this was not just a change of nomenclature. It was very much more than that. During the fourteen or more years that had elapsed since the founding of the Western Buddhist Order many changes had taken place. Not only had Order members increasingly organized their lives round the Three Jewels so that they less and less resembled the upasakas or 'lay Buddhists' of the East; they had also organized their lives round the Three Jewels in such a way that, in the majority of cases, it was not really possible to regard them as belonging to any of the seven different socio-religious classes of persons into which the Buddhist community was traditionally divided. Dharmacharis and Dharmacharinis were simply Buddhists. They were individuals who had gone for Refuge to the Buddha, Dharma, and Sangha and who, as a means of giving expression to that act in terms of their everyday lives, undertook to observe the Ten Precepts. Thus the Ten Precepts were not the Pratimoksa – to use the technical term – of any particular socio-religious class of persons, but represented the ten great ethical principles which all seven classes of such persons had in common. They were what I called the '*Mula-Pratimoksa*' or 'fundamental moral code' and as such constituted, together with Going for Refuge itself, the fundamental basis of unity among Buddhists.

Two years after the transformation of upasaka into Dharmachari and upasika into Dharmacharini I sought to make this clear in section 6 of *The Ten Pillars of Buddhism*, the paper I read to you when we celebrated the Order's sixteenth anniversary. Towards the end of that section I said:

> For the Western Buddhist Order the Ten Precepts, as '*Mula-Pratimoksa*', are in fact the discipline that supports the 'individual liberation' not only of the monk and nun, but of all members of the Buddhist community irrespective of socio-religious status or, in contemporary idiom, irrespective of lifestyle.
>
> Since there is only one set of Precepts, i.e. the Ten Precepts, so far as the Western Buddhist Order is concerned there is only one 'ordination', i.e. the Dharmachari(ni) ordination, which means that in the Western Buddhist Order one is not ordained as a monk, or as a nun, or as a female probationer, or as a male novice, or as a female novice, or as a male lay devotee, or as a female lay devotee, but simply and solely as a full, practising member of the Sangha or Buddhist spiritual community, though it is of course open to one to observe, as personal vows, any of the rules traditionally observed by the monk, or

the nun, and so on. Strictly speaking, these rules are not observed *in addition* to the Ten Precepts but as representing the more intensive practice of one or more of the Precepts within a certain specific situation or for a certain purpose.

Not being a bhikshu, a member of the Western Buddhist Order does not wear the stitched yellow garment of the bhikshu, and not being an upasaka he does not wear the white garments of the upasaka. He wears the ordinary 'lay' dress of the society to which he belongs, though without the implication that because he is not a monk he must therefore be a layman in the traditional Buddhist sense.

Thus from the reduction of the rules comprising the seven different pratimoksas to the Ten Precepts or '*Mula-Pratimoksa*' there follows a reduction – or rather an elevation – of the various socio-religious groups within the Buddhist community to one great spiritual community or Mahasangha. Such a reduction represents a return to, and a renewed emphasis upon, the basics of Buddhism. It can be regarded as innovative only by adopting a standpoint from which those basics are ignored, or from which they cannot be seen for the accretions and

141

excrescences by which they have become overlaid.[25]

21
Ambedkar and
Going for Refuge

From 1981 to 1986 I spent the autumn of each year in
Tuscany, taking part in the annual men's pre-ordination
retreat. In the middle of the 1985 retreat, during the
eight days devoted to the private ordinations, I found the
thought of Dr Ambedkar constantly impressing itself
on my mind in a very powerful fashion and refusing, as
it were, to go away. What could be the reason for this?
I wondered. Eventually I realized that those were the
very days when the 'ex-Untouchable' Indian Buddhists
would be commemorating the original mass conversion, which had taken place on 14 October 1956. This
realization brought to a head a number of things about
which I had been thinking for some time. In particular, I felt I really did want to write the booklet on
Ambedkar and Buddhism to which I had been giving
thought – on and off – for two or three years. I could
now see how it should be done, and towards the end of
the month actually wrote to Lokamitra giving details
of the nine chapters into which it would be divided.
Though I had hoped to start work on the booklet soon

after my return to Padmaloka, in the event I was not able to do so before mid-February and it was not until early September that this latest product of my pen was ready for the press, having grown in the course of writing from a booklet into a small book.

Ambedkar and Buddhism was published on 12 December 1986, six days after the thirtieth anniversary of Ambedkar's death, and launched at a public meeting in London at which tribute was paid to the memory of the great 'Untouchable' leader. In the book I drew attention to the real significance of Ambedkar and the nature of his achievement, looked at the diabolical system from which he had sought to deliver the 'Untouchables', and traced the successive steps of the road by which he – and his followers – travelled from Hinduism to Buddhism. I also studied the way in which Ambedkar discovered his spiritual roots, explored his thoughts on the subject of the Buddha and the future of his religion, surveyed the historic occasion on which he and 380,000 'Untouchables' were spiritually reborn, studied his posthumously published *magnum opus*, and saw what happened after his death. In addition, I gave my personal recollections of Ambedkar. Though the subject of conversion to Buddhism cropped up in most chapters of the book, and though conversion to Buddhism meant Going for Refuge to the Three Jewels, only in one chapter did Going for Refuge feature at all prominently. This was, of course, chapter 7, 'The Great Mass Conversion', which in a way constituted the central chapter of the whole book. In this chapter I not only described the colourful and moving ceremony at which first Ambedkar and his wife and then his followers went for Refuge to the Buddha, Dharma, and Sangha but also attempted to explain the implications of certain aspects of that ceremony.

Ambedkar and his wife took the Three Refuges and Five Precepts from U Chandramani, the oldest and seniormost monk in India, repeating the Pali formulas after him thrice, in the usual manner. Having taken the Three Refuges and Five Precepts from U Chandramani, however, Ambedkar proceeded to *administer them to his followers himself.* This constituted a definite break with tradition – or with what had come to be regarded as tradition. In Theravadin South East Asia, at least, where pseudo-monastic triumphalism was rife, and where monks invariably took the lead on ceremonial occasions, it was unthinkable that a mere layman should presume to administer the Refuges and Precepts in the presence of his socio-religious superiors. Such a proceeding would have been considered as showing gross disrespect not only to those monks who were actually present but also to the whole Monastic Order, and would not have been tolerated for an instant. Ambedkar's action in administering the Refuges and Precepts to his followers himself, instead of allowing U Chandramani to administer them, therefore represented a bold and dramatic departure from existing Theravadin praxis and, indirectly, a return to something more in accordance with the spirit of the Buddha's teaching. Indeed, it represented even more than that; for, as I also explained:

> By [thus] demonstrating that an upasaka no less than a bhikshu could administer the Refuges and Precepts Ambedkar was reminding both the old Buddhists and the new that the difference between those who lived as bhikshus and those who lived as upasakas and upasikas was only a difference, not a division, since all alike went for Refuge to the Buddha, the Dharma and the Sangha. Thus he was, in effect, asserting the fundamental unity of the whole Buddhist spiritual community, male and female, monastic and lay.[26]

That same unity was also asserted in Ambedkar's other break with tradition. Having converted his followers to Buddhism, he was determined to make sure that they would remain Buddhists and not revert to their old ways and be reabsorbed into Hinduism, as had happened once before in Indian history. After repeating them himself, therefore, he also administered to his followers a series of twenty-two vows which he had drawn up specially for the occasion. These vows spelled out the implications of being a Buddhist – as distinct from a Hindu – in some detail. Indeed, in making the vows an integral part of the conversion ceremony

146

Ambedkar made it clear that a lay Buddhist was a full member of the Buddhist spiritual community (thereby asserting the fundamental unity of that community), and that the lay Buddhist, no less than the monk, was expected actually to practise Buddhism. His followers could hardly be expected to practise Buddhism, however, unless they *felt* that they were full members of the Buddhist spiritual community – and, therefore, real Buddhists. This meant that they had to be formally received into that community, just as the monk was formally received into the Monastic Order, and undertake to live as lay followers of the Buddha with the same seriousness as the monk undertook to live as a monk follower. They had, in other words, to take the Refuges and Precepts *plus* the twenty-two vows.

As I worked on my description of that historic ceremony, and tried to bring out the significance of some of the things Ambedkar had done, I became more than ever aware how much there was in common between his approach to Buddhism and mine. Though the saying itself may not have been current in his day, for him, too, commitment was primary, lifestyle secondary, as his contemptuous dismissal of pseudo-monasticism in 'The Buddha and the Future of His Religion' abundantly testified. His assertion, in effect, of the fundamental unity of the Buddhist spiritual community corresponded to my own insistence on the central importance of Going for Refuge, for did not that unity consist in the fact that all members of the Buddhist spiritual community went for Refuge to the Buddha, Dharma, and Sangha, and had not Ambedkar shown that in respect of giving, no less than in respect of taking, those Refuges, monks and lay people were on equal footing? Moreover, in the course of a press conference held on the eve of his conversion Ambedkar made it clear, in response to a question as to which form of Buddhism he would be adopting when he embraced Buddhism, that his Buddhism 'would adhere to the tenets of the faith as taught by the Buddha himself, without involving his people in differences which had arisen on account of Hinayana and Mahayana.' This corresponded to my own 'ecumenical' attitude, as well as to the fact that in the Western Buddhist Order or Trailokya Bauddha Mahasangha (Triratna Buddhist Community) we consider ourselves to be simply Buddhists, in the sense of individuals who have gone – and continue to go – for Refuge to the Three Jewels, and who look for guidance and inspiration to the scriptures and teachings of all the different schools of Buddhism. Thus it was not surprising that on the completion of my chapter on 'The Great Mass Conversion', and indeed on the completion of *Ambedkar and Buddhism* itself, I should have been more than ever convinced that my approach to Buddhism was in line with that of the great 'Untouchable' leader and that the new Buddhist movement with which so many of Ambedkar's followers were now in contact was a direct continuation of his own work for the Dharma.

22
Conclusion

Such, then, is the history of my Going for Refuge. These are the various stages by which the meaning and significance of Going for Refuge became clear to me, as well as those by which, since the founding of the Western Buddhist Order, that meaning and significance has become still more clear, both to me and to others. As I warned you at the very beginning would be the case, in tracing the history of my Going for Refuge I have been tracing the history of a process of discovery that followed, and perhaps continues to follow, a rather erratic course. Indeed, I confessed that my progression here had resembled that of the butterfly, which flutters zigzag fashion from flower to flower, and symbolizes the psyche or soul, rather than that of the hawk, which hurls itself straight on its prey, and symbolizes the logical mind. For this reason some of you may have found this History of mine confusing and difficult to follow. You may even have found it, at times, lacking in continuity, the more especially as the scene changes from England to India, and from India back to England, and I come into contact with Burmese monks and Tibetan Incarnate Lamas, involve myself with the 'ex-Untouchables', write books and poems, deliver lectures, hold seminars and, of course, found the Western Buddhist Order. Nonetheless, if we cast a backward glance over the developments I have described – if we cast a backward glance over a backward glance – I think we shall be able to perceive a definite thread of continuity running through them all.

My Going for Refuge began with an experience of the truth taught by the Buddha in the *Diamond Sutra* and, to a lesser degree, by the Sixth Patriarch in the *Sutra of Wei Lang (Hui Neng)*. As a result of that experience I realized that I was a Buddhist and always had been one, and two years later signalized the fact by formally taking the Three Refuges and Five Precepts from a Burmese monk in London. Being a Buddhist, I wanted to live and work as a Buddhist. This was hardly possible in the army, into which I had by this time been conscripted, and with which I eventually travelled to the East; nor was it possible in any of the various Indian religious organizations and groups with which I became associated after leaving the army. Disillusioned both with them and with worldly life, I therefore resolved to follow the personal example of the Buddha and renounce the household life for the life of homelessness. After 'Going Forth' in this way I spent two years as a freelance Buddhist ascetic, mainly in South India. The experience served to deepen my understanding of the Dharma and strengthened me in my conviction that I was a Buddhist, and I therefore decided that the time had come for me to regularize my position by taking formal ordination as a Buddhist monk. Returning to north-east India, I was ordained first as a sramanera or novice and then, a year and a half later, as a bhikshu or full monk. By this time I had settled in Kalimpong, in the Eastern Himalayas, but whether in Kalimpong or anywhere else being a monk had both its advantages and its disadvantages. On the one hand it meant that I was able to feel fully, and as it were officially, committed to the spiritual life. On the other, it meant that I was in danger of thinking that I was fully committed to the spiritual life just because I was a monk. I was in danger of confusing commitment with lifestyle, as I indeed did do for a while, at least to some extent. Moreover, I soon discovered that in becoming a monk I had become not a 'member' of a spiritual community but only a member of a particular socio-religious group, or a subdivision of such a group, so that an important element – that of kalyana mitrata or spiritual friendship – was almost entirely lacking from my life. Nonetheless, the feeling of Going for Refuge was there underneath the ashes and blazed up whenever the 'eight worldly winds' happened to blow upon me more strongly than was their wont. Indeed, it blazed more brightly and more continuously with every year that passed. This was due not so much to the 'eight worldly winds' as to my increasingly close contact with Tibetan Buddhism, especially as represented by certain Incarnate Lamas and by the Nyingmapa version of the Going for Refuge and Prostration Practice. As a result of that contact I came to have a better appreciation of the meaning and significance of Going for Refuge, that is to say, a better appreciation of the fact that Going for Refuge was not just a formality, nor even the means to the arising of the Bodhicitta, but the central and definitive act of the Buddhist life, of which the Bodhicitta was the altruistic dimension. At the same time, as a result of my contact with the newly converted 'ex-Untouchable' Buddhists, and my taking Bodhisattva ordination, I came closer to seeing that monasticism and spiritual life were not identical. Thus by the time I returned to England in 1964 I had realized that it was Going for Refuge that made one a Buddhist, that Going for Refuge was in fact 'the central act of the Buddhist life, from which all other [Buddhist] acts derive[d] their significance', that it meant organizing one's life round the Three Jewels, and that it constituted the fundamental basis of unity among Buddhists.

In England it did not take me long to discover that, although conditions there were favourable to the spread of the Dharma, a new Buddhist movement was badly needed. A movement was needed that would have as its heart and centre not a society but a spiritual community, and which would be free from the infection of Theravadin pseudo-monastic

152

triumphalism. On 7 April 1968 I therefore founded the Western Buddhist Order by conferring the upasaka/upasika ordination, as it was then called, on nine men and three women; or rather, the Western Buddhist Order came into existence when nine men and three women committed themselves to the Path of the Buddha by publicly 'taking' the Three Refuges and Ten Precepts from me in the traditional manner. The fact that they took the Refuges and Precepts from me, or were ordained by me, meant that their under-standing of the meaning of Going for Refuge coin-cided with mine, at least to some extent. It meant, in other words, that I had in some degree succeeded in *sharing* my understanding of the meaning of Going for Refuge with them, and in the course of the years that followed I succeeded in sharing that understanding, directly and indirectly, with more and more people, so that not counting the three who have, unfortunately, died, and the twenty or so who have fallen away, there are at present in the world 337 members of the Western Buddhist Order or Trailokya Bauddha Mahasangha.

The language of conferring and taking, and even of sharing, should not be construed too literally. It should certainly not be construed in such a way as to suggest that in sharing my understanding of the meaning of Going for Refuge with the twelve original members of the Order I was sharing with them a certain fixed quantity of understanding, so to speak, which thereafter remained unchanged. After the founding of the Western Buddhist Order the meaning and significance of Going for Refuge became clearer to me than ever, and I started to perceive some of the deeper and more 'philosophical' implications of that central and definitive act of the Buddhist life. In particular, I saw that Going for Refuge took place within a context far wider than that of the individual's own personal existence, as well as on a number of different levels. I also saw the full extent of the difference between the 'old' (cultural and ethnic) Going for Refuge, as represented by the vast majority of South East Asian Buddhists, and the 'new' (more conscious and individual) Going for Refuge, as represented by members of the Western Buddhist Order. Eventually, when the Order had been in existence for some fifteen or sixteen years, I saw that the majority of its members had organized their lives round the Three Jewels to such an extent that there was now little or no resemblance between them and the upasakas or 'lay Buddhists' of the East. Indeed, it had become impossible to regard them as belonging to any of the traditional socio-religious categories. They were neither monks nor lay people, neither male or female novices nor male or female lay devotees. They were simply Buddhists, or individuals who had gone for Refuge to the Buddha, Dharma, and Sangha and who, as a means of giving expression to that act in their everyday lives, undertook to observe the Ten Precepts, that is, undertook to observe the ten great ethical principles that in fact constituted the '*Mula-Pratimoksa*' or 'fundamental moral code' of monks and laymen alike. For such 'mere Buddhists' – who were mere Buddhists in much the same way that the followers of the Yogacara school were Chittamatrins or 'mere Consciousness-ists' – a new name was clearly needed, preferably one drawn from traditional sources. First in India and then in the West, therefore, it was decided that in future upasakas should be known as Dharmacharis and upasikas as Dharmacharinis – 'Dharma-farers' or 'practitioners of the Dharma'. That the change of nomenclature should originally have been adopted in India was perhaps not surprising for, as the writing of *Ambedkar and Buddhism* more than ever convinced me, our new Buddhist movement was a continuation of Ambedkar's own work for the Dharma, the great 'Untouchable' leader having, in effect, asserted the fundamental unity of the Buddhist spiritual community no less uncompromisingly than I had insisted on the central importance of Going for Refuge.

This brings me down very nearly to the present day. It brings me down very nearly to the twentieth anniversary of the Western Buddhist Order, which we have gathered in (relatively) large numbers to celebrate. Now that I have traced the history of my Going for Refuge, however, where does this leave me? Where does it leave you? Where does it leave us? Quite simply, it leaves us, in a sense, exactly where we were twenty years ago, or whenever it was that we first committed ourselves to the Path of the Buddha. It leaves us Going for Refuge. We do not, it is to be hoped, Go for Refuge in quite the same way as we did then, or even as we did last year, or last month, or even last week. With every day that passes, in fact, our experience of Going for Refuge should gain in depth and intensity – should take place within a wider context, and on a higher level. With every day that passes we should have a more decisive realization of the fact that we are, each one of us, an arm, or a hand, of that Avalokitesvara who is the embodiment of the Cosmic Will to Enlightenment and, therefore, the embodiment of the cosmic Going for Refuge.

At the beginning of this paper I said that, having traced the history of my Going for Refuge, it would also be appropriate for me to share with you some of my current thinking as regards my own relation to the Order, and the relation of the Order itself to the rest of the Buddhist world. The tracing of that History has, however, taken me much longer than I expected and I shall, obviously, have to postpone my remarks on those subjects to some future occasion. The nature of my relation to the Order has, in any case, transpired to some extent in the latter part of the narrative. As regards the relation of the Order to the rest of the Buddhist world let me simply observe that it is a relation that subsists, essentially, with individuals, and that, on this the occasion of our twentieth anniversary, we are happy to extend the hand of spiritual fellowship to all those Buddhists for whom commitment is primary, lifestyle secondary and who, like us, Go for Refuge to the Buddha, the Dharma and the Sangha, repeating, whether in Pali or any other language:

Buddham saranam gacchami
Dhammam saranam gacchami
Sangham saranam gacchami

To the Buddha for Refuge I go
To the Dharma for Refuge I go
To the Sangha for Refuge I go –

    now, and so long as life shall last
    now, until the attainment of Enlightenment.

Notes

1. Shortly after I had written these lines another friend pointed out that the chart was wrongly drawn.
2. See Sangharakshita, *The Rainbow Road*, Birmingham, 1997, p.80.
3. Bhikshu Sangharakshita, *A Survey of Buddhism*, Boulder and London, 1980, p.xi.
4. Sangharakshita, *A Survey of Buddhism*, London, 1987, p.xv.
5. *Ibid*, p.272.
6. Bhikshu Sangharakshita, *A Survey of Buddhism*, Boulder and London, 1980, pp.xvi–xvii. Also Sangharakshita, *A Survey of Buddhism*, London, 1987, p.xv.
7. Kenneth W. Morgan (ed.), *The Path of the Buddha*, New York, 1956, p.vii.
8. *Ibid*, pp.275–6.
9. *Ibid*, p.276.
10. In the Hindu caste system 'untouchables' were traditionally considered inherently inferior and were excluded almost completely from society. 'Untouchable' as a term is no longer used, many 'ex-untouchable' Indians preferring *Dalit* (meaning 'oppressed').
11. Gampopa, *Jewel Ornament of Liberation*, London, 1959, p.vii.
12. *The Middle Way*, vol. XXXIV, no. 3, November 1959, p.98.

13. *Ibid*, p.101.
14. Bhikshu Sangharakshita, *The Three Jewels*, London, 1967, p.x.
15. *Ibid*, p.150.
16. *Ibid*, pp.225–6.
17. Bhikshu Sangharakshita, *A Survey of Buddhism*, Boulder and London, 1980, pp.xxxi–xxxii. Sangharakshita, *A Survey of Buddhism*, London, 1987, p.13.
18. Upasika Chihmann (tr.), *The Two Buddhist Books in Mahayana*, p.7 *et seq.*
19. Two years later this idea found expression in the dedication ceremony that I composed for the opening of the Triratna Shrine and Meditation Centre, the first home of the newly founded FWBO:
    Here seated, here practising,
    May our mind become Buddha,
    May our thought become Dharma,
    May our communication with one another be Sangha.
20. Sangharakshita, *Going for Refuge*, Glasgow, 1983, pp.21–22.
21. Nyanaponika Thera, *The Threefold Refuge*, Kandy, 1965, p.15.
22. *Ibid*, p.17.
23. *Ibid*, p.25.
24. *Dhammapada*, 168, 169.
25. Maha Sthvira Sangharakshita, *The Ten Pillars of Buddhism*, Glasgow, 1984, pp.38–39.
26. Sangharakshita, *Ambedkar and Buddhism*, Glasgow, 1986, p.139.